Coelacanth

/siləkænθ/

VOLUME 9 — 2020

Published by Newman University

STAFF

Editors   Madeline Alvarez
Matthew Clark
Emily Larkin
Murphy Obershaw
Cole Schnieders
Bri Southworth

Faculty Advisor   Bryan D. Dietrich

ACKNOWLEDGEMENTS

Sister Madeleine Kisner
Jeanne Lobmeyer Cárdenas
Newman University
Newman University Bookstore
Newman University Theatre Department
Newman University Art Department
Eighth Day Books
Sonny Laracuente
John Jones

Newman University is a Catholic University named for John Henry Cardinal Newman and founded by the Adorers of the Blood of Christ for the purpose of empowering graduates to transform society. Newman University does not discriminate on the basis of sex, creed, handicap, national or ethnic origin. Accredited by the North Central Association of Colleges and Schools, 30 N LaSalle ST, STE 2400, Chicago, IL, 60602-2504; 1-800-621-7440. Opinions and beliefs expressed in *Coelacanth* are exclusive to the journal.

CONTENTS

POETRY

ART & PHOTOGRAPHY

PROSE

DRAMA

POETRY

Madeline Alvarez

A FACE LIKE MARS

When the night is dark and breezy
and the sky feels close
you look through glass and see a face
so bright that you feel warm.
It contains many cracks and dips in its ginger-peel skin
as if it had been pelted in someone's target practice.
The flesh is raised and red in some places
yet you discover some that have been left untouched
smooth and soft and golden.
Intrigued, you stay outside for hours, tracing its welts and scars
    with an awestruck eye.
Who knew imperfections could be so interesting?

When you go inside to prepare for sleep
and to scrub your face clean
Mars looks into your viewing glass and sees your arches
like the peaks of his mountains; but you think them too thick.
He observes your crimson clusters, resembling his beloved
    dunes,
which you try to rub away.
He marvels at the mark, made by your illness a few months
    back,
that makes him think of his crater kisses
and your pale tone, shimmering and radiant, which you wish
    was more influenced by the sun.
He wonders at the imprint your knees press into the carpet
and hears your quiet whisper, "God, make me beautiful,"
before you lie down to sleep.

He turns above and prays his request,
"Help her know I'm honored to share her face."

ALL AT ONCE

I'm used to making dents on the backs of my hands,
pushing all the pressure that comes
from the guilt in my stomach through my nails,
and feeling my hands sting and scar as a result.
I try to quit, but it seems beyond me.
Wounds don't just heal overnight.

But you come along on a Friday
and take my cold, hopeless hands between your warm ones
and rub mine into functioning again.
You trace your thumbs over the backs of mine
and smooth away the dents and scars
and worries and fears all at once.
Bringing my fingers up to your lips, you kiss away the sting,
making my hands free to pick up all the love I've stored
behind my fears throughout the years and place it into your
    hands,
which you use to blend affection into mine again.

REGRETTED FREEDOM

Do you have any idea how it feels to be granted this freedom?
Like a caged puppy who begs with her eyes to be let out
only to become fearful when the door opens and she is
    dumped out on the cold, packed earth.
She had longed for the summer when the grass would be soft
    and green
and her ears could fly in the wind as she put as much distance
    between herself
and the memory of the iron bars as could be gained.
But after no more than a few steps,
she whimpers and races back to the familiar place that had held
    her,
even though it would have killed her eventually.
She finds the door shut forever now
and does not know what to do with the freedom she has
    attained.
This world is much bigger than she realized.

RED GROW THE LILIES

Born a virgin October 16
but made completely pure the day after
Maria kept herself clean until the end

Suffering and loneliness were part of her existence
Fatherless at age nine and becoming a mother
to her mother's children at the same time
her mother away in the fields to provide enough to eat
Maria cooking for all the mouths in the family

When she was nearly ten
"Mama, may I go to town and play with Catalina?"
"I'm sorry, my dear, you must stay and watch your sister.
Maybe next year when Teresa is older."

Still, she did her work with love
a little mother to her sister
smiling at the next door neighbor

But he took it too far
"Maria, you're looking beautiful today
The prettiest girl in town, even
How about you lift up your skirt and you can show me
how much more beautiful you are underneath."

"Alessandro, no, I must go in and
get the baby for her nap.
Really. No, let me go."

"One day soon.
Don't tell your mother

or I'll kill her and your siblings and you."[1]

A year later, she welcomed the King of the Universe inside her
"My Jesus, You are my only Love!"

Her mother said
"My darling, today Jesus has claimed you as His
Never offend him, ever."[2]

But the lustful man did not respect this love affair
"Maria, how can you refuse me? It's a dishonor.
A fine young man like me. Why do you reject me?
Do you hate me? God says hate is a sin."
He stripped his chest bare

"No, Alessandro, you mustn't
for God loves us too much to want your way for us."

"Just you wait."
He stormed back to work

At the hour of her Divine Love's Passion
while she was mending the lewd man's shirt
he came in from the barn, wielding an awl
intending to cut the lily from its roots

"Come to me, Maria, or I swear,
you shall feel this instead."

"No, Alessandro, it is a sin, God does not want it![3]
I would rather die than give in!

---

[1] "Maria Goretti - Saint under siege" —Wijeya Newspapers
[2] "Patroness of Purity—St. Maria Goretti, Virgin and Martyr" —James
Likoudis
[3] "Why St. Maria Goretti Was Canonized" —James Likoudis

It is a sin.
God does not want it.
God does not…
He doesn't…
Mama…"

He left long gashes in her stem
but she did not let him fulfill his desire
She remained pure as a lily
though her color was now red as a rose

Teresa's screams brought their mother running
"Baby? Maria! My darling, who has done this?"

"Ale-ssandro…Ma-ma."
The girl could barely be heard
Breathing on through her wounds
she survived a wagon ride to the clinic

"I'm…thirsty."
The moisture gone from her lips
"I need a…drink…please. Water."

The priest came
"Maria, Jesus is asking you to give it up for love of Him.
They can't perform the operation when you
have anything inside."

"Father…then I will…empty my-self
for…my Love."

The doctor entered
"Ay, Maria, my poor girl, we have to work quickly
before the life drains from you.

We have no anesthesia to give you."[4]

"It is…all right.
More to of-fer for…my Jesus."

Halfway through the operation, he begged
"Maria, think of me in paradise."[5]

"Well…who knows
Which of us…will be there…first?"
with an angelic smile

"You, Maria."
Tears in his eyes

"Then…I will
Gladly think of…you."

She clung to life through the night
But in the morning she awoke
on earth for the last time

The priest gave her the Last Rites
"Maria, Jesus died while
forgiving the penitent thief at His side.
Do you forgive with all your heart
your attacker and murderer?"[6]

She looked up with no hint of malice
"Yes!…Yes! I…
For the love…of Jesus,

---

[4] "Maria Goretti" —Dave Kopel
[5] "St. Maria Goretti" —Catholic Online
[6] "Patroness of Purity—St. Maria Goretti, Virgin and Martyr" —James Likoudis

I for-give him, and
I want him to be…
with me one day
in heaven!"[7]

She breathed her last

Her mother wept
"My God, I was not worthy
to have such an angel!"[8]

The townspeople said
"That girl who was killed at Conca
was holy."[9]

Six years later
she appeared on earth
to visit Alessandro Serenelli
in prison.

"Maria? What the devil are you doing here?
Get out, I can't take your condemnation and gloating."

Smiling, nothing came from her lips
But she bore a gift in her hands
One by one, the saint handed him fourteen lilies
He took them and they burned in his hands

He served the rest of his thirty-year sentence in peace
praying to his little angel

---

[7] "St. Maria Goretti and her Murderer, Alessandro" —James Likoudis
[8] "St. Maria Goretti and her Murderer, Alessandro" —James Likoudis
[9] "St. Maria Goretti and her Murderer, Alessandro" —James Likoudis

When he was released
he went to her mother
"Assunta, forgive me.
If I could undo the deed…"

"Alessandro, Marietta forgave you, Christ has forgiven you."
The bereaved woman placed her hands on his face
"And why should I not also forgive.
Your evil days are past, and to me,
you are a long-suffering son."[10]

Together, they received the King of the Universe
into their souls the next day

Alessandro remembered her fondly
"Maria Goretti is really a saint, a martyr.
If there are martyrs in Paradise,
she is the first among them—after all I did to her.[11]
I hope for salvation, since I have a saint in heaven
praying for me."[12]

Now he is blooming, too

---

[10] "St. Maria Goretti and her Murderer, Alessandro" —James Likoudis
(DiDonato, p. 142)
[11] "St. Maria Goretti and her Murderer, Alessandro" —James Likoudis
[12] "Patroness of Purity—St. Maria Goretti, Virgin and Martyr" —James
Likoudis

Meredith Alvarez

DEPRESSION

Sometimes I don't care how I live as long as I die
So disappointed in life I forget how to cry
Telling God He won't love me less, so why should I try
This presumption and despair has invaded my mind
So afraid to move, to breathe, to be alive
Thinking no one cares and I'm someone no one likes
It's so easy to give in, not believe they are lies
Cut myself with a razor is what I think inside
But I know I can't trust intrusive thoughts to be right
I know there's only one in this hard fight
Even though there's tension between the two sides
No one can win if I'm the enemy of mine
Perfectionism captures me with its cocky strides
Discouragement brings me low and anxiety's high
But even now I know God is on my side
And I'll hope in Him, give up both sides of pride
Keep my hand in His through the dark night
Someday I know I'll remember how to cry
And I'll try again to live in the light

Daniel Blake

DAD

From childhood buffoon
To the man amongst the moon
Oh, how I wish I'd be like you
There is more and more they say
Nothingness and tears left come forth dismay
You sat near all with my fears
One day all this tragedy will wash all away
No fear no dismay left on this day
The mind of a boy tragically so gifted
Just one boy with no fear no dismay
You may seek me you may find me
Just to let you know I am here to stay

Matthew D. Clark

A SINKING FEELING

This pit in my stomach spawns
from what is to come,
I hope in long years.

No one knows what is beyond.
Darkness or light or mystery
or all three together.

Life is not life without death;
death is not death without life,
but this makes neither concept
more pleasing.

A cell in the womb
to bones in the tomb.

BLACK BEACH

Suddenly, I simultaneously entered and exited the greatest sleep I would ever have.

My vision was hazy, but not so hazy that I could not see the darkness around me. The sky was black, as if it were painted by the charred remnants of a fireplace. The ground was made up of a coarse sand—each grain as black as a lack of light can be. Had I not understood what it meant to be alive—

I would have assumed I was dead.

And were it not for the occasional puffs of wispy shadows constantly floating by, I would have assumed there was no such thing as life or death at all.

The very blood in my veins was being sucked out by the *nothing*. I had no body,

no soul.

I am cruel to myself in writing "was," "were," and "would." I taunt myself with the very notion that all of this is past tense,
because I am in the present—

my present—

I
am
stuck
in
limbo.

Noble Roman Poet, please save me,

or don't.

In fact,
I pray for hell.

Hell would burn sweetly, taste warm, and feel bright; all such a pleasant contrast to this *nothing*.

I started running. I cannot say why, or what I was running from, or running to—I was just running; my feet picked themselves up on their own, my legs propelled themselves: left, right, left, right. I was running because I could do nothing else.

Usually when one runs, it either feels like they are moving forward, or like the world is moving backward. But I felt neither forward nor backward. I wasn't moving at all—I moved as one would move if their body was void of all movement.

And then I was reminded of the darkness.

Charcoal sky. Wisps of anti-white. Black coast with no ocean. An infinite desert with no lilies. No color. No air,
        no air—
                I couldn't breathe.

Or rather, I could breathe, but I felt no air entering my lungs. My body was entirely deprived of oxygen. And the most horrid feeling overtook my chest as my lungs realized the air was precisely 98.5℉

But I just kept running.

~

At last, all of the running paid off.

I saw a glimmer of LIGHT in the ruinous dune of darkness. This LIGHT was inspiring. This LIGHT was my hope. It was my savior:
                it was a knife.

Its blade stuck up out of the sand. My fingers grasped grains that I could not feel as I excavated the knife. I raised its shiny surface up in front of my face, only to reveal a reflection of someone who did not exist.

Though I longed to savor this moment of *something*, I was too afraid of the *nothing* to stop myself.

I plunged the blade into the left wrist of my strange form.

"Warm blood. Please, warm blood," I whispered, fighting tears that were not present, and in a voice that made no sound;
        but there was no crimson in sight.

Lifeless, LIGHTless, colorless powder fell from the hole in my arm. Not even my blood exists.

I wish I weren't so acquainted with the night. Anti-existing in eternal night. Roaming without roaming in this place that is void of day.

BLACKEST BREW

Said to be the poet's beverage of choice
(alcohol, of course, being the writer's)
coffee is a calm, sweet concubine:
she's there for you when you need her
to warm your lips and help you
think about life.

"Just black," I smile, waiting in line
with the other depressed, sleepless college kids
who could also use a small pick-me-up.
Or a medium. Or maybe even a large.

You know, the strangest thing happens
whenever I raise that paper cup to my mouth,
hesitantly tipping it at a cautious 25° angle
to draw out those first few sacred sips—
steam billowing up like a sauna for my face.
To test the temperature, I enclose my lips
around the opening of the black lid,
hoping that there is enough caffeine
in the geyser of vapor to expedite
the process of my cells awakening.
My mind begins to wonder (or perhaps wander off).

I hear Ella Fitzgerald singing a soul-felt, bluesy song.
I think about how I'm going to make money.
I chastise myself for not taking my chances
with that vivacious girl from Telluride.
I contemplate matters of existential philosophy.
I fear for whether or not I'll leave behind a legacy;
I hate myself for caring so much.
I then wonder if I'm going to care about
any of these thoughts or memories in say, nineteen years—

"Agh!"
The caffeinated concubine interrupts my thinking by biting my
tongue.

Seven minutes pass, and I've eaten enough of my chocolate
muffin to reaccompany its flavor with the black coffee.
It must just be a matter of poetic angst, but that taste,
so simultaneously bitter and sour to my palate,
extracts me from my much too bleak thoughts.
And that heat, well, it warms me in the way
that I wish life would.

Twenty-six minutes pass, and I'm trying to ignore the jitters.

After tapping on my phone an obscene amount of times,
reading some classic literature on my laptop through
somewhat legal means (it says they're public domain),
and attempting some writing of my own,
I kiss the last drops from the vessel and think,
"Until next time, my love,"
and throw the third cup
of the week away.

THE BLIND FLAME

A flame swells within what is sacred.
It creeps across the floors,
up the walls,
to the towers.
Fire has no sight;
only the touch of its destructive limbs.
Swaths of red and orange flow through the building—
torturing wood and stone all the same until it
no longer has the strength to stand.
A precious, astounding, but humble cathedral has fallen.
A holy thing—an ancient thing.
But to the fire,
it was fuel.

Lucas Farney

DOCTOR PRACTOR

I am pain, I am addiction, I am hate.
I am in your room at night,
Keeping you awake.

I know every single one of you,
I know you've all met me,
Although, perhaps not in
This form you can see.
I am genderless, I am endless,
I am the Original Enemy.

I am loss, I am death, I am destruction.
I am the Thing of Horror,
What makes you look over your shoulder.

You'll never see me coming,
Never see me leaving
Just remember the remnants
Of your worst feeling.
Neither black nor white,
I am what you know isn't right.

I am loneliness, I am despair
And I am everywhere.
The Steward of Evil,
Searching and searching
For another soul to steal

I am power, corruption, pollution
I whisper in every politician's ear,
I block the winds of change,
And I'll always be here.

Run, if you want, run, if you can,
You'll never escape my eternal hunt.
I am the shark who smells
Your filthy blood in the water.
Prison guard of your cells,
Ignoring whatever you offer.

I guide your hand as you write,
Make sure the noose fits tight.
You'll fight and you'll fight,
But I'm always the final sight.

Born before Infernal Creation,
I am Fear, Purveyor of
Eternal Damnation.
I hurl asteroids at planets and laugh
At the crumbling nations.

I twisted the American Dream.
My eyes jet black and my teeth, they gleam,
The one who is never what He seems.

Judge of Judas, Friend of Faustus,
Kennedy's Killer, Brutus' Betrayer.
I am the burden on your chest,
And darkness manifest…
I assume you know the rest.

Savannah Kiser

DARK SUNRISES

it all began that night,
when the sun rose high in the night,
deep in the forest air,
they all came to share,
with dark, dark gloom,
their passion began to bloom,
with sweet forbidden love,
it seemed they would fly away as dove[s],
together they planned their escape,
through white clouds of vape,
all they dreamed of was to be free,
but feared the whip, for it stang like a bee,
so they decided to just share the night,
when the sun rose high in the night.

LOVE

is an illusion of utter imperfection,
a bad, bad trip that leaves you in destruction,
just by trying to share half your soul,
you are left alone to wonder as a troll,
seeking for something that doesn't exist,
feels like you're scrolling through a never ending list,
open your lost, lost eyes,
before you're lost within your own demise,
he doesn't even really care,
was he ever really even there?

Kristin Lau

MALAM

I am the meadowlark,
Bewitching is my task,
Keeping you awake in the dusk.

I am the unkind,
basking in the fringes of your mind,
dining on the bits and pieces,
you're so keen to leave behind.

I am the whisper in the dark,
making remarks,
that peer deep into your heart,
I am the thing that goes bump in the dark.

Joseph Mick

DON ROCKWELL

We finished our pancakes
and out the house we raced.
It was time to set out
exploring the creek
like Old West scouts,
going farther than the week
we came across a thousand minnows
in a pond made shallow
by many hot dry days,
the water sucked up by the sun's merciless rays
But recent rains had made the water swell
and the current moved along well.
As backyards turned to fields,
a forest of cattails shields
turtles and snakes from view
forming a fortress too wearisome
to fight through,
we move on after catching one or two.
I was never short of questions:
like what is a Gatling gun?
or how hot exactly is the sun?
Ben always had the answer—
"Look—that's a red-eared slider."

We squinted as the sun climbed
knowing it was probly time
to turn around so we'd be able
to make it back with lunch still on the table.

But the wonder
of what might be
past that bridge
in the waters shaded by the trees
or beyond this bend
wonder was the wind
that pushed us on
as towards new frontiers we were drawn.
There was even
a certain mystery about concrete chunks,
and a few pieces of junk
when they were discovered on an expedition.
Is this where a building once stood?
If only we could ask the ancient cottonwood.
Who would build anything here?
But why move them to this remote spot
where only we walk?

Finally, we turned around,
having covered enough new ground,
knowing we'd be back
but not tomorrow—
we'd head towards the railroad track.
As we trekked to the house,
we'd snag a snake or a snapper
and I'd get some delight
from grandma's fright,
before we took it out of sight.
Or if the fields offered flowers of May
I might get my mom a small bouquet.

The creeks were our domain
On days when the water itself was hot
or days when winter winds came
and it most certainly was not.

Then we would bombard the water's armor
with cannonballs of stone
Or when the cold stayed longer
atop the crick we'd roam.
Perhaps we'd come across a cellar
under the bridge where water froze,
then seeped away,
leaving a remnant that froze again,
Forming a fort under the ice
until we broke the ceiling in.
Season after season,
we'd capture tadpoles, frogs, crawdads, and snakes
but never would we take
the water.
until time
made
it smaller

Years passed and days came
when the three creeks were tamed.
We'd found their end,
or gone as far as the wind
could push us
The only way we'd go so far again
would be to find the pot of gold;
though Colorado mountain cold
streams still seemed
full of life
and the unnamed mountain,
that towered over our cabin
unmarred by trails
managed to fill our sails

Now as I stand on a bridge
that so many times I walked beneath

I try to hear the language
The creek once spoke.
But my mind starts to wander,
there are greater adventures for which I hope.
And I realize that even mountains get smaller
though peaks and falls retain much wonder
and to reach them is an adventure
those wondrous boulders
have lost their magic.
And as I wax poetic
about the stinking puddle below me
knowing everything's sweeter in memory
I wonder why I feel nostalgic?
about such a place.
Though I know that even should I go back
and try to retrace my steps,
I left something there which now I lack.
Nevermore
will I really get to explore
the waters between those banks.
In truth, I had more fun with tanks
and firecrackers in July
And there was nothing better than to fly
a chopper or a plane
in an old school computer game.
But ask one of those old cottonwood
Or my silly old mind:
Here, here were the best days of my childhood.

And yet, there are beaches and caves and certain dirt roads
with wonders even the old can discern
But caves have an end
and beaches are far away
and I drive ever farther from home
because roads are never so good

once they become familiar.

But once in a blue moon,
when the sunlight falls just right
as it trickles into the woods.
Or on that night
when a falling star flashed green
before it exploded
and the moon gave not a gleam
but a million worlds
sparkled beyond my breath
and everything was silent as death
or that time when a deer
stepped out of the night
and gazed at me
so close I
could almost
touch it
adventure finds me.

Ashley Nguyen

AUTUMN THOUGHTS

I walked alone along the narrow path,
the gentle breeze flowing through my hair.
It was cool outside,
cold to me but cool to others.
People say it's because I'm scrawny,
but really it's because
I allow myself to think about it.
It was the season where
I had to wear a thick jacket in the morning
and turn the A/C on in the afternoon.
It's still morning, and
that was okay.

This season was beautiful
with its dying leaves
and effervescent sunsets.
Yet, as the sun rose
and my jacket brushed against itself,
I kept my eyes down.
It wasn't because I feared conversation
—though that were true—
and it wasn't because I was sad.
Rather, I kept my eyes down
because I wanted to crunch the leaves
that scattered around my feet.

Some may think of me rude,
and some may not understand,

but hearing the soft crunch
of leaves beneath my dirty gray sneakers
brings me great joy.
It doesn't take much, I guess
to make me happy
because if the crunching of leaves
was all it took,
then imagine what other little thing
I may do that you may not understand
that could make me happy.

What you may not know
is the disappointment I feel
as I drive through the autumn leaves
and I spot a leaf lying on the road,
clearly dry and brittle.
My excitement builds up
remembering how it felt before
when I crunched those leaves
only to crush not just the leaves
but my young spirit as well
when those ugly rubber tires
from my stupid beat up green car
didn't make a sound
as those autumn leaves crumbled for naught

WONDER

I wonder if anyone in the world
Sees the unnoticed things like I do
Like a falling leaf giving a small twirl
And the flock of geese flying in a queue

I wonder if they see the dying trees
Giving us one last display of colors
Or the spider webs floating in the breeze
And the small ants at war with each other

I wonder if they watch the sun setting
Displaying its rays just like a peacock
Or notice the dull icicles sweating
With each drip falling to the ticking clock

But maybe these people see other things
Because there is so much that this world brings

Leslie Nguyen

CYANIDE

Her solace is in fruit.
Sweetness to a bitter core, yet she persists.
Forcing.
Pecking at something that is
as pit within the stomach
as a seeping poison.
She is greedily asking for more than what is there.
If I could tell her that
if she would take her time
laying it to rest for the moment
Waiting.
For in return, that something might grow.
Knowing all it is worth.

Steven Nguyen

BARE

When I was young I enjoyed my days
Running around on the street
Coming home with bloody feet
Fries and ice cream without delays

I played hide n seek with time
Until it caught up to me
There my shoe laces hung, so lifelessly
But Mom wanted me to find a life sublime

She looked at me all disappointed
"You're late go put on your shoes"
"But Money alone I don't want to choose!"
She still only saw me as a kid.

So I decided to just sit among the trees

Listening to the rustling of the leaves.

Feet bare, callused, among the thymes

Enjoying my poor man's wind chimes

FAR FROM HOME

"Home is where the heart is."
One that contains a good night kiss

A dad to play catch with, a mom to bake cookies
My childhood lacked things such as these

Graduation was a waste of time
And feeling sadness is a crime

But then Uncle Ben got shot, I wasn't there to save him
And Aunt May tries to care for me when it's grim

Friends know me one way, I another,
My personality and feelings remain asunder

With these hands I shoot webs to keep the world intact
Too bad the idea of a family is still too abstract

Mary Jane and Jack Daniels are the only ones with me
A normal life is one I pursue most futilely

"Embrace the suck" is my mentality
And "Save the day" is how it has to be

~Peter Parker

LEVITY

Love is Patient, Love is Kind
Made perfect by Design
Corrupted by the world, turned into lies
However, fixed within your **eyes**

SOUL ORCHESTRA

A beautiful instrument that only she can play
It's a living song and harmonizes with the melody

It follows a beat, a rhythm…
It speeds up and it skips
It communicates without words
A foreign language only two understand
A Morse code that only she can decipher

It's vivid like a painting with brushstrokes of gray and yellow

It can be as quiet as a whisper in the wind,
Or as loud as thunder during a storm in late spring

But like the things of spring, it awakens from its winter slumber
Everything surrounding it blooms and the orchestra begins to

play.

My heart speaks, paints, and plays for you.

Murphy Obershaw

HANDS

Dry, red, cracked,
bloody, burning, itching,
sandpaper hands
in the winter.

Lotion, aloe, cream,
balm, Neosporin, Vaseline,
oily hands
trying to heal.

Oranges, lemons, limes,
water, Germ-X, Lysol,
fiery hands
never going to heal.

IF I TOLD YOU

If I told you that I liked you
Would you turn and walk away?

If I told you that I liked you
Would you sit right here and stay?

If I told you that I liked you
Would you say that's not okay?

If I told you that I liked you
Would you feel the same way?

If I told you that I liked you
Would our friendship decay?

If I told you that I liked you
Would this be your favorite day?

If I told you that I liked you...
Maybe I won't tell you.

No, not today.

PARTNERS

I didn't mean to
It just kind of happened
Nat and I are always together
Going on missions
All over the world
Taking on all kinds of threats
Just the two of us
It's what we do
We're partners

I don't know what happened
Maybe it was seeing her in action
Man, can she knock 'em out
Maybe it was her long hair
The way it bounces when she walks
Maybe it was when we met
And all I wanted to do was say "hi"
But this is not what I should be thinking
We're partners

Just for the record:
1. I didn't plan this
2. It's not my fault
3. It could be worse—
She could have liked me back
Now there's a thought...
But at the end of the day
None of that matters because
We're partners

Crap.
Half of S.H.I.E.L.D probably knows
Everyone here is a spy after all

I wonder if she knows…
That could screw everything up
Fury definitely knows
He knows everything about our lives
But he hasn't separated us yet
We're still partners

I'm the archer
Why was I the one shot in the heart?
And why did I have to fall for her?
Nat is so amazing,
But she's also kind of scary
They call her The Black Widow,
And it's for a reason. Yikes.
Maybe I should be thankful
We're just partners

WHAT IS LOVE?

What is love?
Love is storge
Love is philia
Love is eros
Love is agape

What is agape?
Agape is self sacrificial
Agape is a gift of self
Agape is chastity

What is chastity?
Chastity is about the beloved
Chastity is putting them before yourself
Chastity is doing what's best for them
Chastity is not just abstinence before marriage

What is marriage?
Marriage is a Vocation
Marriage is a sacrament
Marriage unites you to someone forever
Even though people get divorced sometimes

Then who do you marry?
Someone you love?
But what is love?
How do you know who you love?
How do you know when you should marry?

You just know…
At least that's what they tell me
You just seem to know who you love
And who you should be with forever

Then what is love?
Love is patient
Love is kind
Love protects, trusts, hopes, perseveres
Love never fails

Love is not just a feeling
It is so much more
Loving someone is loving
Them beyond feelings of passion

How do you know you're in love?
Maybe one day I'll know for certain
Maybe one day I'll just know

Lauryn Ogden

HOLLOW HEART

scraping the edges of an empty heart
scared that someone else will tear it apart
for nobody knows that nothing is left
oh how it used to be, he is a theft

I may forget, but my heart refuses
because you're the one that my heart chooses.
My heart turned black from the poison of love
leaving me feeling like hearts have been shoved

WITHOUT YOU

The thought of you makes me mourn
my faint memory of your hand on the transmission
the smell of cigarettes when we entered your car
I would run to your car after my half day of school
I could always tell something was off
but I never knew it was true
everytime I hear someone mention suicide
my heart aches at the thought of you
no one really knows that I am without you
it is hard for me to have your name roll off my tongue
I have been without you for so long
people stroll past me every day with your features
I just want to hug them for our last time

Machen Olson

BREAKING THE CYCLE

A young impressionable teenage girl going on thirty
Headstrong, know-it-all, oblivious to her many faults
Nothing was as it appeared
Blinded by the fantasy of a Beauty and the Beast fairytale
Fraudulent love exploiting each gullible thought
So easily manipulated with imaginary dreams of family
Entangled in a web of desire
Distorted illusions of a now fragmented psyche.

Hearing that I should have not made him mad
The unrealistic notion that he hit me because I was bad
Fictitious promises that it will never happen again
Willing to overlook the obvious red flags and patterns
Avoiding eye contact so no one would become suspicious
Internal conflict, the battle to stay or to leave
Fear drowning confidence as it gasps for air
Cowering to my abuser as he put me in my place.

Cringing at the thought of being a damsel in distress
Long after the bruises faded, the nightmares still haunt me
Constantly lying to oneself regarding the lapse of judgement
Allowing the pain and torment to immobilize me from moving
    on
Then saying "NO MORE" to being a victim, his victim
Declaring liberation from the chains that kept me shackled in
    terror
Turning concrete to build my wall strong enough to keep
    people out
No longer in need of a prince to save me, I saved myself, I
    survived.

YOU CAN'T GIVE UP

They can knock me down
They can beat me up
They can see me as a clown
No matter what I can't give up!

My teardrops will drown my face
As my future seems black
I fall apart in this space
No matter what I can't give up!

Hope may seem bleak
Beset with personal strife
So distraught unable to speak
No matter what I can't give up!

I will stand against whate'er comes my way
I will fight against any naysayers
I will endure through the end of the day
No matter what I will not give up!

Corby Redington

FOG

Broken rays
Piercing
Thinwhite blinds
Shatter on haze
And smoke.
Morning.

So drifts
The aroma—

Thick arabica mud,
Incense burning slow,
And cigarettes—
Pungent sweetness
Smoldering in a pile—
Their own ash.

Nicotine buzz lingers.
Tendrils of loose smoke coil.

Drink percolates along,
Brownblack sludge,
Steeping, scorched earth.
The caffeine soup,
Finished and mugged,
Steams.

Cole Schnieders

BEAUTY'S BURNING

Is it so wrong to long for immolation?
To dream of those hot, splintered timbers
Crushing me like a warm, weighted blanket.

It is a reminder, sure, of the temporary nature of Beauty.
The falling spire, vaunted high over Paris
That once inspired a reviled creature to embrace
The corpse of a roaming, passing beauty.

It is a reminder, too, of the dreams of logical men.
How the spark of a careless worker
Ignited an ununited world
More surely than rational rage against the ecclesial.

It is a reminder still of the dangers of ill-crafted beauty.
All I create, crafted as surely as lead-sheathed beams,
Will melt like poisoned wax,
Leaving a desolation worse than if never sawed.

Is a bonfire of refuse any less noble than the immolation of
    Notre Dame?
Why add a verse to the matchbooks of libraries?
Why chase an Ideal that is always fleeing?

I long to burn, if only to cauterize the wound of living.

FIGHT, FLIGHT, OR DIE

Sure, if you beat a dog,
it'll learn —
Learn to hate itself for giving in.

Before you call an ambulance, trust me, I've been there:

400 dollars to tell a doctor the same truths
        that I'd tell anyone, if only they asked.
40 dollars for the pleasure of pissing in a cup
        despite promises that I've done nothing harder than
           Advil.
100 dollars for a guard to watch me on CCTV
        then take my clothes anyway.
And 200 dollars that I don't have
        just so I'll think:
only one way out.

But why these dreams of a stronger rope,
Furrows made just right, no, straight,
Sighing for a plant so snide,
Or a bag being sufficient fixation?

Why not run and hide, bark and bite?

Run to be lashed
With words wounding then salted?
Bark to be muzzled, chained,
because "good dogs don't scream"?

Of course, it doesn't *mean* anything,
just another emotion to push aside,
But this one? So morbid and shunned?

I think because it is:
fight, flight,
or die,
and I could only ever
pick one.

INSTAGRAM

I hope what she sees in that red heart
Is that I love her,
      or at least the idea of her;
that I miss her;
that I should never have let her go —
      even if in the moment,
      I saved her
            from
      my own
            downward
      spiral;
I hope she knows the heart is
for her smile;
for memories of her;
her internal and external beauty that, so far, I've found
    irreplaceable.

I THOUGHT I HAD TO BE EMBARRASSED

I thought I had to be embarrassed
that my dad did the work that no one else would
embarrassed that he had to set dozens of alarms
that would drive my mom mad.

When he'd come to get us from school
I'd never want him to come inside
because everyone would know
how he made a living.

I was embarrassed that he snored everywhere:
during scout meetings held in metal folding chairs,
at football practice, reclined in his truck,
and even at the table after making dinner.

I thought I had to be embarrassed
that he didn't always know how to help with my homework
or that he wasn't available to read us bedtime stories,
even though he was the best at it.

I thought I had to be embarrassed
when I told him I was giving up a white collar job for the
    white collar
and, worse still, when I left that,
for empty words that might not feed a family, like he did.

He was never embarrassed.
He wasn't embarrassed when I called him "sanitational
    engineer."
Nor when I told him he stunk.
Or even when I called him a big, dumb idiot.

Instead, unabashed,

He hugged me with warm callouses
entrusting me the future he built
by lugging other people's garbage.

Kaitlyn Smith

DOVE

I think to myself as I clear their plates
How fascinating it is that we can make such a mess
And in an instant, all traces of us can be wiped away
Everything is cleaned and left in pristine shape
As if we were never here

Sheridan Sommer

WRECKED

Day bleeds into nightfall
You were the only one to call
Pain surrounding all my being
Thought running from you would be freeing

Never saw the car coming
All I've been doing lately is running
Running from my family, you and life
Running away from being your wife

Heartache is a familiar pain
Hurts less than the glass in my brain
As my vision blurs, I see your face
All I needed was a little space

Flying up into the sky above
Knowing what we had was anything but love

Katie Stanford

SUMMER

Dangling lights sway gently
underneath the stars
      in midnight's breeze

Allison Williams

GREY AREA

My opinions are too loud,
      But my voice is too soft.
My ambitions are too lofty,
      But I am too short.
My beliefs are too deviant,
      But my behavior is too meek.

Tell me, how can I, at once,
Be too much and not enough?
How can I be nothing I am
And everything I am not?

I speak too much or too little.
My energy is "intimidating" or "dead."
I sing too boldly or too quietly.
Nothing is ever black and white
Except, apparently, when it comes to me.

But I am blissful and I hear them not,
      As Dante Alighieri would say.

I will do the things no one can imagine,
Even if no one imagines anything of me.
I am too much, not enough.
Too loud, too bold.
Too meek, too small.
No matter, I am proud of what I've made.

The time is now to create my legacy.
I will create my immortality.

In the words of Walt Whitman,
"I am larger, better than I thought;
I did not know I held so much goodness."
The world is mine,
       And it is dying.
       And it is open to life.
In these messes of lives in this mess of a world,
How can anyone expect to be perfect?
How can anyone settle to be mediocre?
Vague, afraid, a chameleon to opinion.

I choose instead to be beautiful.

HEALER DOES AS HEALERS DO

Just so you know that you are not alone:
I will bring tape when you begin to break.
I will be Atlas when your sky begins to fracture,
When the shards start to fall.
When the walls start to close in,
I will wedge them apart so that you can breathe.
I will hold you until the dawn
Just to see the sunlight shine on your breathing form.
Safe.
Secure.
Not going anywhere.
I will never leave you to tackle your darkest moments on your
    own.
No, I will always be there.
Just so you know that you are not alone.

WE'RE ALL EQUAL IN THE END

Death does not discriminate.
The Grim Reaper does not prefer a gender.
Shinigami do not care about your ethnicity.
Fatality does not have a favorite number.
Death is random.

Death is inevitable.
We try to avoid it but it always,
Always rears its ugly head,
And rings its bell to signal the end.
Death is unpredictable.

Death can be a last resort.
A final choice, the end game.
Those who seek it are reckless,
Those who avoid it don't know how to live.
Death is aloof.

Death is a finish line.
"You've completed the race,
Now you get to rest awhile.
Say what you will to your adoring public,
I'll carve it in stone for them to see.
Now sleep in your wooden box
        Six feet deep."
Death is black and white.

Death is closure.
Murder is revenge.
Suicide – a choice.
Illness – a chance for light to shine on the mourners.
Death is mercilessly forgiving.
Death is only the end if you think the story is about you.

Nathan Yeager

BUBBA

Late into the night we sat on the cliff's edge.
The reservoir stretched out before us, deep blue
cutting through a wooden landscape,
trees swayed fifty feet below, the stars and half moon above,
below broken cliff shards sat at the water's rippling edge.

They each sat at my side.
My legs dangling over the granite
ledge, its ridged surface coarse
against my bony butt, I
felt the chill night wind weave between my toes and
gently flap my unbuttoned flannel.
We were silent, the night was not—
the underlying hum of cicadas flirting in the dark, leaves
bustling, black wings calling
from the sky, the water below kissing the jagged shore.

I grappled with the sudden urge to lean
forward, to join nature's symphony,
to rest with the empty beer cans we used as golf balls,
but they held me at the ledge.
The smell of Chance's cigarette, so sweet to a young addicted
        mind,
a warm pull from the handle of Jack Daniels passed by Paul,
        and
a drunk Timmy racing through the woods
looking for firewood, he'll settle for half a decaying tree, we see
his head lamp dancing between the branches,

Beyond the reservoir's moonlit waves a storm bellowed, tiny
     threads
of lighting flash as if the gods were taking portraits.

TARGET AT 7:40 A.M.

The crowded morning sky shimmered,
long purple clouds
around a fuzzy orange ball
of gas some millions of miles away
slinging photons across
her unmasked face and
into her eyes to see a world so
average and bleak in her own
time.
In the back of that old Nissan truck,
our DNA mingling on the
wooden tip of our third Black and Mild, we
had talked about everything from
her dreams of being a secret agent to
her hatred for some queen on HBO.
With my notes sprawled around
the truck bed floor, she quizzed
me on Roman history. My exam
in four hours.

The parking lot was empty, save for
those coming in for an early shift
hoping to catch their worms, only
to be flanked by a middle-aged
white lady screaming about expired
granola bars.
We walked past her on our way
to the makeup aisle, then to
the back for a half gallon of peach tea.
With it we toasted the near-empty lot,
to the end of that night we marched
together, and to the start of our separate
days; she to pour coffee at the nursing home,

and I to dwell on the fall of
empires.

ART & PHOTOGRAPHY

Clock and Mirror

Marissa
Kucharek

Perfume Double

Marissa
Kucharek

The Other

Marissa
Kucharek

Typology of Glass

Marissa
Kucharek

Window

Marissa
Kucharek

Cyanide

Leslie
Nguyen

Brilliance

Steven
Nguyen

Lost

Steven
Nguyen

The Farmhouse

John
Suffield

The Match

John
Suffield

Butterfly

Hadassah
Umbarger

Butterfly on Chives

Hadassah
Umbarger

Flower

Hadassah
Umbarger

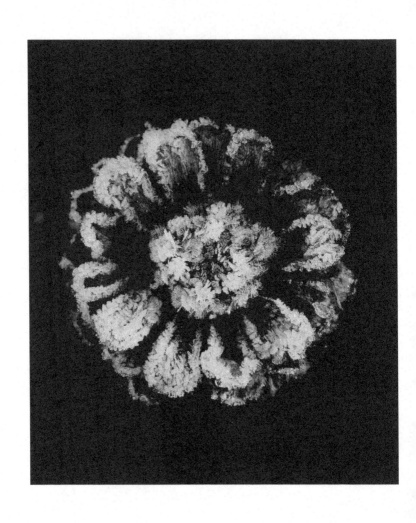

Frost

Hadassah
Umbarger

Happy Cat

Hadassah
Umbarger

Water Droplets

Hadassah
Umbarger

PROSE

Madeline Alvarez

THE WEIGHT OF A NAME
(Inspired by John Updike's *A&P*)

"Julie! Baby, I need you to do something for me before you go."

Cynthia, Patsy, and I had hardly stepped off the porch before my mother's voice stopped us in our tracks.

I was always embarrassed when Mother called me nicknames. I'd known the girls for just a few weeks since Mother and I had moved to Gloucester after she and Daddy had divorced, and I didn't want them to think I was still a kid like Mother did. Back home in Syracuse, my best friend Cristy would have chided me.

"Are you going to let her talk to you like that?" Cristy would roll her eyes and toss her head. "Lord have mercy, Jules, you're almost sixteen! If my mother ever called me 'Baby' in public, I'd be so humiliated, I'd die on the spot."

When I'd first met Cynthia and Patsy, I had thought my best tactic to fit in would be to take on Cristy's attitude. I didn't have half her sass, but I had expected the girls would be like her, and I figured it wouldn't hurt to blend in. But these new friends of mine didn't say much when Mother called me nicknames. Honestly, they didn't speak much at all, and without meaning to, I had become the queen of the group.

"What now, Mother?" I tried to sound annoyed, but I was still getting used to talking to her like this.

However it sounded, it didn't phase her. "Baby," she said, coming out of the house. "I need you to head down to the A&P and buy some herring snacks for my guests." She pressed a dollar into my hand and turned to go back inside.

"Mother!" I was shocked at her suggestion but hoped the girls would hear my protest as irritation. "We can't go like this. We're already in our bathing suits and about to head to the beach." Maybe she hadn't noticed. She could be so blind sometimes.

She turned back just as the screen door swung shut behind her. "Oh, that's all right, sweetheart," she said, peering out. "I'm sure no one will mind." Before I could object further, she had disappeared into the laughter that filled the house.

"Uh, we can wait here for you, Julie, if you want to go real quick," Cynthia said after a moment. Her arms were crossed and her hands clutched her elbows. Patsy nodded and shifted on her feet, making her cheeks jiggle a little.

I could have thrown on some clothes over my swimsuit, jumped into my car, and been back within ten minutes, herring snacks in hand. But instead, I chose to use the opportunity to assert my new power.

"No, you girls come with me. It will only take a minute." I started walking to my car at the end of the driveway, not looking back to see if they were following. I had always followed Cristy when she'd expected me to.

Seconds later, I heard the sound of the girls' feet slapping against the burning concrete. We got into my car and drove for a few streets without saying anything. I was technically a few months too young to own and drive a car, but Daddy had given it to me as my early birthday present with some of the money he'd won from the lottery before Mother and I had moved away, and Mother had not enforced any rule about me waiting until I got my real license to drive it.

After a minute of riding in silence, I decided to be a bit vulnerable with the girls as a way to thank them for coming with me. "Want to know which boys I think are cute since I've been here?" I described guys I'd seen on the beach or in town, asking the girls if they knew any of their names.

In my rearview mirror, Cynthia and Patsy looked at each other and giggled.

Cynthia said, "I think I might know one. His name is Max Auden, and he should be a junior with us when school starts."

"Hopefully I can get to know him before then," I said.

The girls giggled again.

It wasn't long until we reached the store and parked, and then we looked at each other with a flutter in our stomachs. But I put my shoulders back and tried to look like I'd gone into the store in my bathing suit a thousand times before.

"Come on," I said. I hopped out of the car and pushed into the grocery. The two followed a few steps behind.

The store was busier than I would have thought for a Thursday afternoon. The girls tried to hide behind the racks at the ends of the aisles, away from the shoppers' shocked looks at the sight of teenagers in bare feet and bikinis waltzing into the store. Although I hoped my friends wouldn't notice, I was self-conscious, too. I mean, what had Mother meant about no one minding? Had she not noticed I'd had the body of a grown woman for the past three years? She had been so busy with the divorce and the move and now with her parties that it wouldn't have surprised me to find out she hadn't.

I could only guess what the A&P customers were thinking. I wasn't trying to show off like I could picture Cristy doing. Truth be told, I'm sure she would have thought to prance through the store in her bathing suit whether or not her mother had asked her to.

What made it worse was that I didn't know which aisle the refrigerated party snacks were in. I asked the girls but they mumbled that they didn't know. I don't think their families had money for things like that. The only reason Mother and I did was because of the lottery money Daddy had to split with her when he won it during their divorce. The judge had ordered him to give half his winnings, ten thousand dollars, to Mother. I was still getting used to having so much. And not having him.

It wasn't until we were in the frozen section and I saw my reflection in the frosty glass that I noticed my bikini straps were down. The swimsuit I had on was a bit too big. In fact, it was my mother's. I figured she wouldn't notice it missing, since she had about half a dozen now. This one was my favorite. It was almost a skin pink color and had little squiggles all over it. I thought it complimented my flaxen hair. I reached up to pull the strap back onto my right shoulder but stopped when a woman pushing her toddler in a cart walked past me and my friends and made a comment under her breath. Something like, "Girls today. Where's their shame?" I decided to leave the straps, just to spite her.

"Should we ask someone for help?" I asked the girls when we had walked down almost every aisle twice. I was getting cold wearing nothing but a two-piece in the air-conditioned store. If I caught a cold, I was blaming Mother.

"But..." Patsy started, her eyes wide in what looked like fear.

"They're all men," Cynthia whispered, glancing over her shoulder.

They had a point. But we were going to be there forever if we didn't do something soon. I looked around and noticed a man about my daddy's age behind the meat counter. "Let's ask him," I said, deciding he was our safest bet.

"C-Corner of the back wall." The man stammered and pointed in response to my inquiry.

"Thank you," I said. We hadn't thought to go down that way again. Whoever decided to keep the herring snacks in the same section as the yogurt obviously hadn't been thinking, either.

We reached the section, and I bent down to get the jar. When I straightened up, I saw Patsy whispering to Cynthia. They looked at me with unease written on their faces.

"What?" I looked back and forth between the two of them.

"Um, the guys at the front are…staring at us," Cynthia managed to get out. "Patsy saw them."

Patsy nodded, looking like a chubby child. It seemed as if nodding was the only form of communication she was capable of having with me.

At first, I felt ashamed, and my heart dropped to my stomach. But when I looked towards the front of the store and saw the two younger guys ringing up groceries at the registers, my heart jumped. My friends and I had hurried past them when we'd walked into the store, but now that I was paying attention, I saw that one of them was one of the boys whose name I didn't know but who I'd been talking about in the car. Both cashiers were looking our way and whispering to each other but stopped when I looked in their direction. Since they were men, I was sure that whatever they were saying couldn't have been as rude as what the woman who'd passed me earlier had said, even if it was probably something vulgar. I hadn't ever been aware of anyone checking me out before and I felt kind of flattered. I wasn't even wearing makeup. It was like a confirmation that I had grown into a woman at last. I wondered what Mother would say. Not that I would ever tell her. On an impulse, I put the money I had been holding into the top of my bathing suit between the crease in the middle and walked to the front of the store. The girls followed me, and I pictured their faces, mouths open and eyes wide. I knew they would have said something to stop me if they hadn't been so shocked.

The store was almost empty by then. I began to hesitate when I realized I hadn't thought through which one of the guys to go to. Should I approach the one I thought was cute, or the other one to make him jealous? But an older man pushed past us to the second register, so I led the girls toward the first, not missing more than a step.

"Hi," I said when I reached the slot. My voice was so quiet that I wasn't sure the guy had heard me. I cleared my throat and just smiled instead, handing him the jar.

He smiled back, hardly taking his eyes off me as he rang up the herring snacks.

"That will be 49¢," he said, then waited to see where I would produce the money from.

I almost chickened out and said, "Oh! I forgot the money at home." But I took a deep breath and pulled it out of my swimsuit top, handing it over to him. The look on his face made me want to laugh. He just stared with his mouth open.

Then, out of nowhere, a man came and stood in front of me at the end of the checkout slot. "Girls, this isn't the beach," he said, disapproval written all over his face.

The reality of the inappropriateness of my actions began to set in. My mind raced to think of what to say, and then, even though I knew it wasn't right, I decided to bring my mother into it. "My mother asked me to pick up a jar of herring snacks." I tried to sound innocent.

"That's all right," the man said. "But this isn't the beach."

My face felt hot, even though my feet were still cold on the rubber-tile floor. I bit my lip and tried to keep from crying.

"We weren't doing any shopping. We just came in for the one thing." It wasn't Cynthia's voice I heard. I turned and saw Patsy, looking as if she were going to faint from the effort of speaking aloud.

"That makes no difference," the man retorted. "We want you decently dressed when you come in here."

I felt shame at his words, but more than that, I felt anger. For some reason, Patsy's little speech had given me courage again, and I challenged him. "We *are* decent."

"Girls, I don't want to argue with you. After this come in here with your shoulders covered. It's our policy." He turned away from me and looked at the guy behind the counter, who was still holding the jar of herring snacks as he looked back and forth between the warring sides. "Sammy, have you rung up this purchase?"

Sammy. I finally knew his name. But a lot of good it did me then.

Sammy mumbled something, and opened the cash register with the touch of a button, smoothing out the bill before putting it on top of the ones. He handed me my change and took his time putting the tiny jar into a giant paper bag, twisting the bag as if he were afraid I would hold it the wrong way and make the jar fall out.

This was the final blow to me. He could have just given it to me, and if it had broken, it would have been my fault. But no, he kept on twisting it, like he was patronizing me.

"Poor kid," I imagined him thinking. "Did she think I would fall for her with those thin legs and tiny chest?"

I wanted to get out of there. I snatched the bag from his hands before he could twist it anymore and marched toward the exit without checking to see if my girls were following. On the way out, I heard Sammy say something, but I didn't have the courage to see if he was talking to me. Besides, I had tears running down my face, and I couldn't bear for him or anyone else who might have been watching the scene to see.

I opened my car door and slid inside, burning my legs on the leather seat. But I didn't care. As soon as I heard the back car door slam, indicating that Cynthia and Patsy had climbed into the backseat, I pulled onto the road and sped away from the store.

"Will you drop us off at our houses, Julie?" Cynthia was once more the spokesperson for the two of them. "I'm sorry, but we don't have time to go to the beach now. We promised our mothers we'd be home by suppertime." She didn't offer a word of comfort.

I didn't say anything through my tears but gave a nod I thought both the girls could see in the rearview mirror. Even if they couldn't, I figured they'd see they were home soon enough. They lived right next to each other a few blocks nearer to town than where my mother and I lived, so it wasn't out of the way for me to take them since I had to pass by there anyway before arriving home.

The girls didn't look at me when I pulled up between their houses. They got out of my car and flew up the steps to their own porches. As I drove away, I thought I saw Cynthia's mother behind a fluttering curtain, but I didn't stay to find out.

***

I saw Cynthia one more time that summer after the incident. I walked up her driveway a few days after we had been to the A&P, but she met me before I could set foot on her porch steps.

"So," I said when she didn't say anything. "What have you been up to?" I wasn't sure if I should apologize for my behavior at the store or not. And even if I was sure I should have, I wasn't sure I would have done it. The whole thing had been so humiliating and I didn't want to bring it up again.

"Nothing much," Cynthia said, rubbing her toe in the dirt and around the sharp stones of the gravel driveway. She had her arms crossed as usual.

"Where's Patsy?" I asked. Almost every time I had come over before, she could be found on Cynthia's porch swing, but I didn't see her then. "I was wondering if you two wanted—"

"My mother said I'm not allowed to talk to you anymore," Cynthia said all of a sudden, lifting her gaze off the ground and staring right into my eyes.

I was too stunned to say anything for a second. "I—"

"Patsy's mother, too. So I guess this is goodbye." The girl turned away from me and walked across the yard to Patsy's driveway. Once she reached her friend's porch, she gave me a last glance—the same look the woman in the A&P had given me. Then she opened the screen door to Patsy's house and let herself inside.

The stones dug into my bare feet as I left the driveway. Hot tears stung my face, and I let them. As I passed through town, I couldn't help but notice the women pointing at me and whispering behind their hands. On my way to Cynthia's house, I had thought they were still talking about the "new girl." Now I could guess what they were really calling me.

As I pounded up my porch steps and slammed the screen door, I realized I would take my mother's nickname for me over the name the women had called me, any day. Better to be Mama's "Baby" than the town's "Slut."

Matthew D. Clark

EARTH & AIR

He stared into his computer. A blinking cursor and seventeen unopened emails. The office was quiet. He was quieter. A conversation between two coworkers began. He listened at first, then zoned back out. All the while, his eyes remained on that blinking cursor.

Suddenly, his mouth opens involuntarily and he spits up a beetle. A very strange beetle that had spewed out some strange liquid. He feels sick, sitting there on a red decaying leaf of the rainforest's floor. There, twigs, fungi, and grasses create quite a curious carpet. Sweet, humid air fills his little lungs. This is the type of air that could come from a green mountain, but probably came from an island, and in reality, comes from a dense, tree-choked jungle.

The frog isn't sure where he came from, or what he was daydreaming about. All he knows now is that he is hungry.

"Maggie," said Ricky. "Who do you think is gonna win the Super Bowl this weekend?"

"Well, I'm clearly hoping it's the Chiefs." She indicated her jacket with one hand and poured herself a cup of coffee with the other.

Water.

He isn't hungry—he's thirsty.

Hopping around for a minute or two, he rather quickly happens upon a flower full of water. It is like a holy grail to him. Manna from heaven. A lily in the desert.

Except it isn't. He is simply an amphibian, and it is merely water.

Most excited, he leaps into the flower, immersing himself in the life-inducing liquid. "When one finds water, why not bathe?" The frog remembers that old proverb from somewhere.

As one need is met, the other becomes stronger. It is now time for the frog to hunt.

"Fred," Ricky began. "How's the sale going?"

"Which one?" Fred laughed.

He opened nine of the seventeen emails. Four were work-related, one about an alumni reunion, two were from his bank, one from his lawyer, and one was from his wife.

"Steve!" Ricky snapped. "Working hard or hardly working?"

The office erupted into laughter.

"Hey," Steve protested, "I made three sales this morning. Now all I can think about is lunch."

He misses. If he had only caught that fly, he would've felt so much better. He's so hungry.

So he hops, and he hops, and he hops. Searching high on the brown branches, and low on the fungal floor—the frog is determined to find food.

He remembers a simpler time: a time when he was a tadpole. Swimming around in a clear brook, blessed by the gentle waves from a waterfall much farther upstream. Wandering around without a care in the world. Exploring the rushing river as if it were new. It was.

And again he remembers that old proverb: "When one finds water, why not bathe?"

Another fly escapes.

Then he recalls when his legs were functional at last. How he stumbled around at first, eventually teaching himself to hop properly. What an accomplishment. Hopping about the lush Australian rainforest as if it were new. It was.

There goes another one.

Now he reminisces on that incredibly rainy March last year, when he found love for the first time. Except it wasn't "love." He is a frog, and to reproduce is to reproduce. There was nothing special about that day which he recalls so fondly. Three-hundred bright-eyed tadpoles swimming around, probably one-sixth that survived—if he's generous—and about this time they are also learning how to use their legs.

And another.

"Maggie," Fred beckoned. She got up from her cubicle and went over to his. "Did you hear that Steve met up with Jennifer last night?"

"What? I don't believe that for a minute," she crossed her arms.

"No really. Mike said he saw them at that fancy Italian restaurant when he was there with Madison."

"I don't believe it. She's happily married to—"

"Keep your voice down! These walls are paper-thin."

Another.

The frog has missed five flies in total.

Hopping about some more, the frog moves on from flies, and decides to try his luck at beetles again.

"Ricky," Maggie motioned, peeking into his office.

Ricky followed Maggie to her cubicle.

"Did you hear about Steve and Jennifer?"

One beetle goes by.

"What about Steve and Jennifer? I've already heard the joke about them at the Christmas party."

"I'm serious, Ricky. I think Jennifer is cheating on—"

"No. I don't believe it," Ricky held up a dismissive hand.

"That's what I said. But Mike saw them when he was out on a date with Madison last night."

A second beetle.

He finished opening and reading his emails. The sixteenth was another from his lawyer, the seventeenth, another from his wife. His face contorted as he hesitantly began filling out the document.

And a third.

With tears in his eyes, he submitted the document.

Instead of finding a nice place to sit outside and enjoy the weather while he ate—like he usually did—he sat in his chair and ate his microwave dinner silently.

Steve walked by and decided to stop at his desk. "Lighten up a little. You look like your cat died." Steve patted him on the back and sauntered off.

After texting his wife, he excused himself to the bathroom.

Hunger takes over. The treefrog dies. It can no longer remember that old proverb.

Minutes pass, and a menacing tarantula creeps out from underneath some dark green foliage and sinks its fangs into the frog. It realizes he is dead and moves on.

Hours pass, and a brightly colored bird swoops down and picks up the frog's corpse with its beak. Realizing he is dead, it moves on.

Days pass, and a venomous-looking snake slithers across the red leaves and snatches up the tiny dead carcass, but immediately spits it out and moves on.

Weeks pass, and the fungi finally decide to have their feast. The brook flows. The trees rustle. The birds chirp. An orange-and-black beetle crawls across the forest floor.

And life moves on.

Ashley Nguyen

WHITE LILIES

It was a cloudy September day as signs of fall slowly crept onto a peaceful, secluded town. Greens were withering to rustic red-oranges, littering fields with a beautiful dying scene. As the leaves broke away from their branches and drifted onto the brown grass, a hunched figure hobbled through the forest path. It was an old man crushing groups of leaves with each step of tattered leather shoes. The sound echoed through the empty fields, away from the daily commotion of town. Occasionally, a crow would cry out, temporarily drowning out the crisp crunch of leaves.

Clutched in the paper-thin hand of the old man was an array of vibrant colors; a bouquet of exquisite flowers displayed with blues as clear as the undiscovered skies and purples as mystifying as the night atmosphere. In the other hand he held a smooth, worn cane, feebly attempting to alleviate stress on his knees and back. The man's tainted coat flowed through the wind as he reached an opening in the trees, revealing a cemetery with a corroded black fence on the perimeter. As he approached the front gate, two middle-aged women passed by, smiling courteously when they recognized the familiar man visiting the graves once again. Upon entering the cemetery, the sun decided to make an appearance, sending a wave of heat through the cool breeze. A robin gently passed by the man and gracefully landed on the grave he was visiting, though it flew away with the approach of the sound of leaves. Gently placing the array of flowers upon the mound of dirt topped with a dreary gravestone, the old man sat at the end of the grave and waited patiently. After a breeze blew clouds over the sun once more, a sort of ghastly fog morphed into a young woman who seemed to be in her mid-twenties. She was dressed from the time of the civil war, elegant yet gentle. Her eyes fell over the flowers, and then to the man, and a melancholy smile reached her lips. After a brief introduction between the two friends, the woman continued with her story from their last visit. Her body suddenly sprung to life as she explained the fierce battle that occurred, describing it with great detail. He latched onto every word, transforming them into individual figures that were shouting, shooting, shaking with adrenaline. Exotic colors danced behind his closed eyes; imaginary gunshots rang through his alert ears. Every aspect was a reality to the man until the woman suddenly disappeared and silence ensued.

The figure paused for a while, enjoying the serene, midday atmosphere before standing and returning to the long path home. Nearing the town, more townspeople happened to pass by, and each one greeted him with a warm smile and the occasional small conversation.

He returned home by the time the sun descended and the moon ascended. His shabby leather shoes were positioned at a place on the floor where dust avoided. He placed his tattered coat upon the coat rack by the freshly lit fireplace, leaving a smoky scent to linger for the next day. He laid his cane to rest on a table where a small meal of bread and cheese were consumed. When he finished all that was necessary, his head laid to rest on a lumpy pillow and drifted off to continue the story with a wild imagination, a smile lingering on his wrinkled face.

The old man went out to collect flowers before the sun rose the next day. Rather than collecting blues and purples, he collected whites as pure as pearls freshly polished and ready to sell in the market, and reds as crimson as a child's cherry cheeks. Both of the colors were bold enough on their own, but mingled together, they united to create a stunning bouquet, catching the eye of anyone who passed by.

He waited for the daily delivery of cheese from the little neighbor boy before beginning the long, timeworn journey to the cemetery. Many townspeople passed by, each sharing their kind, loving smiles to the figure who they all knew so well. They would occasionally exchange greetings or offer a bit of their produce, and he warmly accepted them all with a smile and a wave of his brown cane.

When he reached the graveyard, the atmosphere was different. The air was more morose; the sun wasn't shining and the air was colder. Looking throughout the graveyard, the old man spotted the source: a funeral was being held. There, over a fresh mound of dirt, stood a small group of five dressed in black including a little girl who cried silently. Alongside the group, an opaque, suspended spirit of an adolescent boy cried loudly.

The old man slowly approached the scene, waiting for the group to leave before acknowledging the wailing boy. The ghost didn't notice for quite some time, but the old man patiently waited until the boy shed his last tear before noticing and greeting him. The boy, shocked that someone could actually see him, looked from the gentle smile on the wrinkled face to the beautiful array of flowers clutched in his delicate hand. Once more, the boy sobbed, running toward the old man with every intention of embracing him, only to find himself running right through his body. Gathering himself, the boy sulked back to his grave and sat there, crying into his knees.

With a sad smile, the old man placed the flowers on the fresh grave before sitting next to him. The boy then lifted up his head, greeted him once more, and began to tell the tale of his wasted life. Images of thievery and murder flashed through the paper-like eyelids of the man. After some time, the group of five came back to visit the grave again only to find the old man crying through his closed eyes with a bouquet of flowers lying next to him. The group couldn't help but give a wistful smile seeing someone who cared for a criminal like their deceased.

The adults gossiped amongst each other about how they would see the old man visiting the graves every day with fresh flowers and talking as if there were someone listening, but the little girl who was crying silently earlier didn't want to hear what they were saying because she too could see the boy's spirit. They finished their gossip as the boy faded away and the old man was once again left in silence, revering over the boy's tragic life. There wasn't much left to do except to stand and go home.

The path home seemed darker than usual and there were fewer townspeople walking about. The setting sun was also covered by clouds, darkening the rest of the way. Even so, he made it home with time before the moonlight could emerge from the horizon and break through the clouds. The tattered shoes were once again placed in the place where, strangely enough, a small layer of dust had gathered. Disregarding the small fact, he placed his tainted coat on the coat rack and tried to light the fireplace but found nothing to start it. Moving on, the old man decided to skip the small meal, leaving the cane behind to sleep on the lumpy pillow which felt much softer this night than any other night. Even through all the strange events taking place, leaving the figure in the cold, he drifted off to sleep with a smile resting on his wrinkled face.

The sun decided to appear much earlier than usual the next day, awakening the old man with a warm heat wave. The field of flowers seemed to have many new flowers blooming, creating a beautiful assortment of flowers reflecting off the sun's rays. A slight breeze roamed over the field, causing the flowers to dance elegantly. If only he could stay like this forever! But alas, he had to visit a grave today, so he grabbed a single white lily and headed off to the graveyard.

The town was quiet today; calm and still from the usual bustling of commerce. It was peaceful, but on a lovely day like this the children should be running around with their companion of a pup or another child, laughing and singing merrily. The old man just brushed it off, continuing on the long journey. Finally reaching the cemetery, he realized why the day was quiet indeed. The whole town had gathered for the funeral of another deceased, but there was no mourning spirit to be found. Curious, he walked toward the open grave, yet to be closed in by dirt, and peered inside. A sudden wave of frosty wind reached him as he saw himself, lying lifeless inside the casket. He looked around to see if anyone was as shocked, but they were all looking down, some crying, others closing their eyes, still others whispering a prayer of best wishes. A familiar group of five was also there, with the little girl being the only one staring straight at the old man. In her hand, she held a white lily, similar to the one that he was holding, however, he found himself empty-handed. The cane and flower were gone. Not only that, the tattered coat was replaced by a new, flawless suit and the tattered shoes were replaced with shiny black ones.

Aware that no one else could see, he accepted his fate and crawled into the casket, arranging himself to lay where the body lay. The little girl peered over the spirit and placed the lily by his gravestone, smiling at the peaceful body that lay inside as she stepped back. The spirit rested his head on the soft cushion of the casket, closing his eyes to drift into an eternal slumber, a smile lingering on his wrinkled face.

FAIRY TALES

The door creaked as it opened. A crevice of light spread across the floor until it illuminated a good portion of the dark pantry. A man wearing full armor stepped inside and peered around the corner. The pantry was filled with barrels of apples, potatoes, and carrots. Wheels of cheese and bottles of spices sat on shelves amongst other things. As he took a step forward, his foot hit a breast plate. There were pieces of armor littering the floor surrounding a curled up figure under a blanket. He made a path for himself and sat down. He stared at the blanket for a moment and then tore it away.

The closed eyes of the person underneath shot wide open, and she looked at him dead in the face. "What do you want?" she asked.

The man sat there for a second, not quite sure what to do. He had planned out what he was going to say before he came in, but after staring into her bloodshot eyes and watching the tears and snot roll down her face, he was at a loss for words.

"You know that can't protect you if it's on the floor, right?" were the only words he managed to say.

"I don't think armor can protect me from this."

"Are you okay?"

Her eyes narrowed. "Yeah, Imma let you figure that one out on your own."

"Do you want to talk about it?"

"Talk about what exactly?" she said while wiping the snot from her face. "How I was stupid? How I probably made a fool out of myself? How I thought that maybe, just maybe, life could actually end up like a—" she stopped and looked down at the floor.

"You thought that maybe if you tried hard enough, life could end up like a fairy tale," he finished. She continued to look down at the ground without saying a word. "I don't want you to feel stupid for what happened."

"But I do."

"These things just happen."

"Don't talk about it." She pulled her knees close to her chest.

"It was really sweet though."

"I said don't talk about it!"

"Okay, okay. Take a deep breath. I won't say it."

She tucked her head back into her knees. "Is that all you wanted to say?" the muffled voice said. "Are you finished now?"

"You're an adult who was hiding under a blanket in a dark pantry. I have a lot more words I need to say to you."

"Alright. Go on."

"I just want you to understand that you shouldn't feel like you did something wrong. You were doing your job. I know you care so much about people and protecting them from harm. You would not be a royal knight if you were not an expert defender. I just never realized that you cared *that* much about him, but there is nothing wrong with that."

"I can think of a few reasons why that's wrong."

"Oh, really?"

"Yep," she said while lifting her head. She counted out the reasons on her fingers. "One: I am a knight. He is a prince. In fairy tales, the knight always gets the prince or princess, but in the real world, that apparently does not happen. Two: Everyone adores him while I'm just another warrior. I have to fight battles and be there for him, his loved ones, and all the people that adore him. I defend, I protect, I guard, and do whatever needs to be done to keep them safe."

"You care. You really care about everyone you need to watch over," he interjected.

"Three," she continued, "people like that don't just fall for people like me."

He sat there for a moment and sighed. He placed his hand on her shoulder and looked into her reddened eyes. "Stop. No more looking at yourself like you're a piece of trash. If a prince doesn't like you 'that way,' then you shouldn't look down on yourself for that. He may be a prince, but he is still just a guy. There are lots of guys out there, and one of them will love you the way you should be loved. He may not be a prince, but he will treat you like a princess. If he doesn't, I will come find him, and we will have a conversation about how to treat a lady."

"Dear gosh. That is the most terrifying thing I have ever heard you say."

"Thank you. You know, life is not a perfect fairy tale, but you can still fall in love with someone. I mean, you'll probably fight sometimes or one of you could snore. But, if you are with someone you truly love, it will still be the greatest thing ever. Do you understand?"

"I just can't believe you used that word after I asked you not to say it."

"Aw, well, you'll get over it," he patted her on the shoulder and stood up. Then, he held out his hands for her, and he pulled her up. "You're going to be okay."

"I always am."

"Good, now clean this place up. That is some quality armor you have scattered all over the place. Clean your face up too. That is the most pitiful looking thing I have seen in my entire life."

"Thanks for the pep talk," she said sarcastically.

"Anytime," he replied. "Gotta make sure my fellow knights are functioning enough to do their job and not hiding from the world in a dark pantry," he added while exiting the room.

She bent down to pick up her armor and slowly put it back on. After she exited the pantry, she washed and dried her face. Not a single tear remained as she left the room and walked back to her station.

"Hey, wait," a familiar voice called from behind.

She swallowed the remaining fragments of her pride and turned around. "Yes, Your Majesty?"

"I'm glad I ran into you. We need to discuss the security detail for the parade tomorrow."

"All the details are already worked out. You don't have to worry about anything."

"You're the best. What would I do without you? Anyways, I'll see you tomorrow."

"See you tomorrow, sir," she replied with a slight bow and walked away. She started to pass another knight who gave her a high five.

"Nice social interaction," the knight said.

"My soul hurts." If only her armor could protect that too.

Zowie Riedel

HOW YOU HURT ME

SIX

At age six, you made us move three times. I watched you bring different men into our house while he was deployed. I woke up to a random stranger that would take us to the lake or to get pizza. I watched him yell at you when he was home. You'd fight and let him hurt you and us. You got pregnant with twins and got divorced again. That was when we moved the third time, and still you made irrational decisions. I found cigarettes in your purse one day and stole them. Of course, you found out. I watched you kick my grandma out, and she was crying on the porch. My childhood was spent watching you tear apart relationships with husbands, parents, and your kids. At that time, I knew I didn't want to be like you, ever.

SEVEN

At age seven, we moved to a different apartment and you had your twins. That was when I first experienced anxiety without knowing what it was. You left us all in the car: your seven year old, six year old, and twin boys of only a few months. You ran inside the store, and the boys started to cry. I didn't know what to do, and I started crying too. A car parked next to us, and the people inside were looking in our windows. I didn't know if they were going to stop the crying or take us. I hid my face in Jeremiah's car seat, knowing he had no idea what was happening. It was the only thing I could do. They started talking on their phones and I could hear the man say that there were four of them in the car, alone. I knew he meant us and I was scared we were all in trouble. When you came back, I cried and told you what had happened. Then you drove us out of town to a man's house. We stayed there for the night, and I really thought you were in trouble. He took us to the park and let us eat fast food in the car. In December of that year, you gave us up…all of us. The twins were adopted by Aunt Brenda all the way in Texas, while we were sent to Kansas with our dad. You had gone off with a boyfriend to Alabama. I told you I hated you, and I was never going to take it back because you ruined my life.

NINE

At age nine, I was starting over again. My new stepmom was probably worse than you in some ways. She was manipulative, a liar, and more than completely unfair. She would brush our teeth with soap and make us stay outside all day. I only saw you for Christmas that year, and I remember telling my whole class that you were going to be with me. I was more than excited because I had missed you. Instead, you told me that you were getting married and were pregnant again. I was more excited to have a baby in the family but less excited because I wouldn't even get to be with you or the baby. You ended up having her three months early, and she was so tiny. I didn't get to see her for a few months while she was in the hospital because they thought she would die. Luckily, that was the last kid you had, and she did survive. The first time I held her, I said she felt like a little baby doll. She was more precious than gold in my eyes. I told you I was sorry for ever saying I hated you because I was stupid and didn't mean it.

TWELVE

At age twelve, my great-grandpa died. He was your grandpa, and I loved him more than anyone. He told me before he died that the secret to a "forever marriage" was to simply say "okay" instead of arguing about meaningless problems. The twins came to the funeral and called me "sissy" or "cuzzy," and I didn't know how to take it. They were my brothers. That year, three other people died, including my great-grandmas on both sides of the family and a kid from my school. He was on a four wheeler with his cousin and they hit a tree that split his head open. I went to his funeral and saw him in his casket with bruises all over his face. I guess everyone thought that it was part of life to experience these kinds of things, so that was why I did. In December of that year, you moved to Nebraska to be closer to me. You were still eight hours away, and it seemed pointless to me. Your new husband's family was all in Alabama, and we had gotten to love them. Twelve was also the last time I got to see your dad, my grandpa. You pushed him away, and he never spoke to us again. He had gotten remarried and you were upset that he had a new wife and kids and family, but you never cared how we felt when you did the same.

THIRTEEN

At age thirteen, my dad got divorced around the time of my birthday. Later that summer, I came to see you for two whole months, and, in that time, my dad had gotten a girlfriend. Three months later, they got married, and I had three new siblings. I hated all of them, and now there were six of us and a new evil stepmother. I always blamed you because it was clear to me that you couldn't keep a relationship, and I honestly assumed the same thing would happen with your current husband. If you were a better person, then you might have still been married to my dad. You were still in high school when you had me, so I knew that was your first mistake. You hated any stepmom I had, and I knew you were jealous because you would ask me about her and her kids all the time. You took me driving around and made me cry because you said I never wanted to see you and I liked my step family better than I liked you. Thinking about it now, every time you hurt me like that it was because you were being selfish or jealous.

FIFTEEN

At age fifteen, I was a freshman in high school and was consumed with my own world. When I wouldn't reach out to you, then you wouldn't reach out to me, and it was still my fault. You had my brother convinced that he needed to come

115

live with you, and, if he could stay out of trouble, then he would move there. On October seventh of that year, my friends all told me that something was wrong with my brother and I needed to talk to him. A guy in my class told me if I didn't talk to him about something he had done then it would be too late. I planned on talking to him that night, but he had a friend over, so I waited. Before I knew it, it was too late, and somehow everything had spread around the school: he had been recording us when we were showering, dressing, and all without us knowing. One guy had made a website and sent a link to everyone. It was like something out of a movie because of how unreal it was. When I got home from school the next day, my stepmom was throwing his shit onto the driveway and cursing at him. My dad drove him all the way to you, and you didn't even know what was going on.

SIXTEEN

At sixteen, my dad said we needed to give him another chance and visit him for a weekend at my grandpa's house. Dad was always big into family; maybe that's why you didn't work out. It was June, and we had decided to go swimming and go hiking. While in the pool, he kept touching Avery and me, and we didn't even think anything of it until later. When we got back from swimming, I went to shower, then he did, then Avery did, and that was when she realized his phone was casually sitting on the shelf next to the shower. He had done it again, and we lost our minds. I said he needed to go to juvie, but dad wouldn't let him. Avery and I just spent hours shaking and crying. He broke everything I had, and again you didn't give a fuck. He was the only real sibling I had, and I felt used and betrayed. I have never come to your house since then, and I never plan to. You always found ways to say it was my fault or I was overreacting. You said that you knew how I felt and I needed to learn to forgive. Our relationship has been completely fake and horrible since then.

116

EIGHTEEN

At eighteen, I told you not to trust him around my six-year-old sister, and you said he wouldn't do anything to her. That showed me how little you thought of me and how much your stupid self believed in him. I had found out that there were investigators in your house, seeing if it was a fit environment. They wouldn't be doing that without cause, but still you told me everything was fine. You threatened to not go to my graduation because you said I didn't want you as my mom. You said I was childish for caring if he was around and that you didn't have to be in my life, either. To this day, you still try to make me see him. Now it has been seven years since I've seen my grandpa, and you're trying to push my grandma out of your life now, too. You rarely talk to me unless you choose to bring up drama or find something to argue about. Constantly, you talk about everything you've done for me, but as far as I'm concerned, I am more self-sufficient than anyone my age. You say you're proud of me for wanting to be a surgeon and for working three jobs while being a full-time student, and of course you would be. But you'll never be proud enough to just have me as your daughter through everything.

SMASH THE CAR

I slammed the door shut behind me. That was petty, and I heard Mom yelling after me to come back and close it correctly. Whatever.

I pulled the shed door open a little more carefully, though. The door was old, and I had enough things to fix. My sledgehammer was leaning against the wall. Frayed duct tape wound around the skinny handle; it was extra assurance that the head wouldn't fly off mid-swing. I bent over and grabbed it near the head. Easier to carry that way.

Mom had come outside and was still screaming at me. Then she saw the sledgehammer. "Derrick, drop the hammer and come back inside."

I swung the handle up, its grip familiar. It was so light, really. The lump of shaped steel at the top was only about twenty pounds. Mom just started crying and stopped yelling.

Back when I was young, younger than I am now I guess, school would hold its own Halloween thing. A way for kids to be safe and not eat apples with razor blades in them. Mom stayed at home to pass out candy, worried about tricks. Dad would turn me and Jaime loose after loading us up with tickets for all the games scattered around the school. Then he'd go off by himself and we wouldn't see him until the end of the night.

Anyway, they had one of my favorite activities, Smash the Car. A junkyard in town would donate a shell of a car. They'd remove the windows and taillights and stuff so there wouldn't be shrapnel flying all over the place. Then they'd hand kids with no coordination a sledgehammer for three minutes. The first time I saw it, I was in second grade. They wouldn't let me try; it was only for middle schoolers.

I traded a friend all my tickets for his bag of candy and watched from the school's steps. Bang. Bang. Bang. Whatever you broke off, you got to keep. I watched older kids walk off with side mirrors, an antenna, and I even saw someone's dad walk away with the trunk lid. I don't think anyone was really trying to get mementos, though. They just liked hitting something and winning for once.

I didn't get my chance to try until seventh grade. Technically, sixth grade is middle school, but Mom wouldn't let me go that year. That year was the year Jaime was a sophomore, and mom found her passed out in the bathroom, drunk. It was Jaime's way of getting back at mom for not letting her go out to a party. Mom was cool with parties, usually, but she hated Halloween. Something about not knowing who was behind the mask made her worry more than normal. Jaime's night turned out alright, relatively. The party got busted before anyone could get as drunk as she did.

Seventh grade year, though, I begged mom to let me go. She agreed as long as Jaime could take me so she could stay with the house. Jaime dropped me off and told me to walk home when I was done and to call her boyfriend's house in case of an emergency and to not tell mom. I didn't care; I was too excited for my turn.

I bought my own tickets and everything, then sat and watched like every year. I knew there would be a point the other kids would get tired of it. Then it'd be me and the high schooler roped into running the show. I handed him an August's birthday worth of tickets.

The teen said, "Go to town, kid. Hell, you can go all night unless someone else wants a turn."

I crossed the "Do Not Cross" tape they strung around the car. The guy handed me the goggles and showed me how to use the hammer.

"You want to lift it high and let the hammer fall with gravity," he said. "If you get good with it, you can start aiming. The pros, like on railroads and stuff, use their whole arms to make it go faster down. One shot, they can drive spikes longer than your face into railroad ties faster than you can blink."

I nodded, and he held out the hammer. I took it and almost fell over. The thing only weighed ten pounds, but I still remember how heavy it felt.

The teen ducked out of the ring and gave me a thumbs up. I took a deep breath. The mirrors were already gone, the passenger door too. I didn't want a trophy. I wanted to destroy that damn car.

It took me a while to get a rhythm going. Like I said, that hammer was heavy, and I could barely lift the thing over my head. I swung. I swung. I swung. I swung. By the tenth swing I was locked in. I couldn't stop.

Smash. That. Damn. Car.

"Shut up!" I screamed. I hit it again. "Shut up!" I had started using my arms, my back, my legs. I swung with everything I had. I was breathing heavy now, sweating. "I hate you!" The hood buckled. I kept swinging that sledgehammer. I needed to win. Just once for Christ's sake.

"Hey. Hey. Hey!" Someone was yelling at me to stop.

I kept going. I needed it out of my life. I yanked the hammer high, just barely holding on.

"Hey, kid!"

I screamed with a final ferocity and I slammed the hammer down. It punched right through the hood of that car.

There was a hand on my shoulder. I dropped the hammer and turned. I tried to collect myself, but I know now that my eyes were bugged out, and I was covered in my own spit and sweat. My hands were blistered and every muscle ached. My head hurt and my ears were ringing.

"Shit, son, you alright?" It wasn't the teen who had stopped me; it was a man in mechanic overalls. He looked the car up and down. "Shit."

The hood was bent into a V, covered in dents, and had the hammer sticking upright out of the hood like Arthur's sword in the stone. The high school kid kept staring at me, like I was gonna go after him. I took a few more deep breaths.

"I'm okay, thank you." I ducked out of the crime scene tape and started walking home.

"Hey, kid?" The man in overalls had jogged up to me. He was black, with white hair and a fuzzy white beard. I stopped and faced him, tensing for him to start yelling. Sticking out his hand, he said, "I need you to work for me. What's your name?"

"Uh, what?"

"That was the most impressive thing I've ever seen," he said. "I'm the guy who donates the cars every year. I've got nothing but lazy nephews and baby grandsons now, and, well, I could use your help."

"Well, I'm Derrick. I gotta go home before it gets any darker, my mom is gonna worry." His hand was still sticking out, so I shook it.

"Well, Derrick, I'm Happy." He grinned with cigarette-smoke yellow teeth.

"Um, well, Mr. Happy, you can call my house tomorrow. It'd have to be okay with my mom." He took the number and didn't even write it down or ask for it again. He repeated it, said it backwards, and then nodded.

"Next Saturday, Mr. Derrick, you'll be seeing me. Don't you worry, your mom and I will work it out."

Somehow he convinced my mom to let me out of her sight, and he came the next Saturday in his rattling Ford pickup to take me to work. He showed me what needed done, and I did it. He dropped me off after dark with an ice cream cone, twenty dollars, and a thank you. Mom was impressed and made me go back. Pretty soon, I was waiting on the front porch steps every Saturday morning for him.

We would do odd jobs around town, like mowing and painting houses. Happy worked for free on Saturdays, helping family, friends, and strangers where he could. He always paid me, though. He'd tell me about his life when we drove around, and I'd tell him about mine, and he'd listen.

When Dad left the first time, Happy brought me and Mom a different meal every night for a month. When Dad left for the second time, Happy helped me talk to the police and the lawyers. When I turned sixteen, he sold his father's mint-green '55 Chevy pickup to me for a hundred dollars. He taught me how to drive it and how to take care of it.

I drove to his place every day after school to break apart beaters with a sledgehammer. Sometimes I'd take a customer out and help them pull the part they needed. After dark, Happy and I would sit around and talk. One night he said, "Mr. Derrick, I want you to know that you're a man. I'm proud of you, son."

Happy died of a heart attack before he could, "see my prom sweetheart in Dad's old truck." He died before he could see me graduate. He died before Jaime's wedding and her baby girl, Joy. He died before I went to college. He died before tonight, when I got a call from my mom that Dad was back.

"I'm over this, Mom."

She stood there shaking and shivering in the October night air. I walked around to the front of the house. He was sitting in his '71 Firebird, flicking the brights off and on, smoking a cigarette. He saw me.

"Derrick! Mom told me you got a new truck. Nothing like my baby girl, though." He revved the engine and flicked ashes my way. I kept walking. "And you graduated. You're going to college, too, that's my boy. Going to do me proud one day." He saw me but didn't see the sledgehammer. "Where's your sister? Mom said she got knocked up or something. If there's one thing I hate, it's—"

I slammed the sledgehammer into the only thing he ever cared about.

Adam Steffens

SINDBAD SINGS THE BLUES

My fingers danced absentmindedly with her dirty blonde curls, and we spoke of dreamy things. The sunlight was fading and the sky through the screened-in window in her ceiling was a molten orange, streaked with clouds and the shadows of clouds. She wanted to be a mermaid, she said. She wanted to swim to islands in crystal blue seas and lie on a white, sandy beach until her tail dried up, and then she would walk along the pristine shores and squish the sand between her toes. Though beaches were yellow, she supposed—not white. I remarked that many beaches were indeed white, and the sand would most certainly squish between her toes. She giggled at this, and sat up on her elbows. Was it true? White beaches? When were you there? I shrugged and began a recollection of years at sea. Tramp steamers and titanic freighters. I pointed to a painting she had made on the wall above her wood stove. It was a white beach, with a turquoise sea and crude palm trees like yellow crescents topped with emerald green fronds.

"See those trees there? They bend like that in heavy winds," and I told her of a hurricane I witnessed in a fishing village south of Mindanao. "There—that one? With the dolphins?" My finger traced a waving line of black dolphin shapes that were rising and falling out of some blue waves that were the sea, painted across her cupboard. I described the way they swim and how they will follow ships. She laughed at this with such glee that I couldn't help but laugh too.

It was times like this when I felt at ease. My wandering mind was at rest, and I could just sit back and enjoy her happiness. She would smile as big and bright as she could, and her teeth would dazzle in the light of the fading sun. She was older than me, this half-mad angel. Older by half, at least. She had deep laugh lines from her incessant smiling, and her skin was a ruddy bronze. Freckles dotted her face like the islands dotted the sea, and sometimes I would just lie there and daydream that I was some ancient mariner, studying the dots on her skin like the marks on some pilot's map. She never seemed to notice, so busy was she in telling me of her latest treasure she rescued from some salvage yard or condemned home. Or else she would be painting the walls of her piecemeal houseboat with more pictures of islands and beaches and palm trees.

She had never left the Mississippi, she told me. She had never felt anything but mud between her toes. I didn't pry about her life. I knew right off that a woman like her was entitled to her discretions, and a living such as she made could not have come without sorrows. I had seen the thin, white trails of scars on her lithe form when we made love and there were times when I caught her staring emptily out the window at the great, muddy brown river swirling by. Her knees would be tucked to her chest and her chin would be resting there—with her arms locked tight about her—and I could just see the years and the tears and the sadness. As soon as she noticed me looking, she'd perk right up and that big smile would flash across her face. Sometimes her eyes would blaze, and the oranges I would be eating would have to wait.

This evening, my stories had dried up early, and I had fallen silent and glum.

"I miss the sea," I said. "I miss the ships and the adventure." She curled up closer and snaked an arm across my belly.

"I came ashore after six years, and here I am—twenty-two with a roll of money in my hat that would last me months yet, but for what? The city is bustling, but it's hot and miserable, with hot and miserable people. People hate each other here.

They'd just as soon spit on you as look at you. I hate it." She adjusted her body so that her chin was resting on my chest and I looked down to meet her gaze.

"Then why are you here?" she asked.

Why indeed.

"Because I'm a man grown, and I need to act like one. I need a home and a family. I can't live on the sea forever."

Her voice was flat when she said that it sounded like I had a home and a family—out there on the sea.

I barked a cynical laugh and shook my head. "You wouldn't understand," I said. That was a mistake.

She pushed off my stomach hard and straddled me. Her eyes glittered like glass in the dimly lit cabin and her voice was hard as flint. "You think I wouldn't understand?" she said, her voice quivering. "You think I didn't have a mother who wanted children and a husband for me? You think I wanted to live in a broken-down hovel on the river? I've had to claw my way through this life, and rip and tear and nail it back together with my own two bleeding hands!" Tears were running slowly down her hollow cheeks and the pain she must be feeling was suddenly dwarfed by my own shame and guilt.

"You have everything," she said softly, her anger subsided. "You have me. But you aren't happy. I…I know that you'll leave me. I know you'll go away eventually, and I'll be here again. Alone again. You have your memories of white sandy beaches and blue seas and…and dolphins, and I'll just paint another picture." She stopped momentarily, and seemed to breathe with such evenness and depth that the very air around us became still and heavy.

"But I'll be happy. I have what I have, and I have found peace in that. I'm not sad or ashamed about who—and what—I am. I'm just mad that you think I wouldn't understand. I've been thinking these things and understanding them as long as you've been alive, mister." Her edge was gone. She sniffled quietly and rubbed her nose. There it was.

"I'm sorry," I said. "I'm a bastard."

She nodded sharply. "Yes. Yes, you are."

She laughed then, and I smiled and pulled her close. The waves of the river rocked us to sleep and in the darkness, I dreamed. I dreamed of crystal blue seas and white sandy beaches, and maybe…just maybe, there would be room for two.

DRAMA

Clayton Norris

All Will Be Well

CHARACTERS

John Conrad	A wounded soldier left for dead on the battlefield. Has a powerful desire to live and return to his life back home.
Death	The Grim Reaper. Believes it is John's time to die and has come to take John's soul to the afterlife. Is extremely manipulative in his tactics. Is played by three different actors as he takes three different forms, appearing as Ben, Ron, and as a classic grim reaper.
Liz	John's girlfriend back home
Ron	John's hated next door neighbor
Hanks	The leader of John's squad
Mercer	A squadmate
Dillon	A squadmate
Enemy	A French medic who offers John aid but does not speak English.

SETTING
The entire play takes place in the middle of a muddy trench in the middle of a battlefield in rural France.

TIME
Modern day. In the midst of a war between the United States and France.

Scene One

(The lights come up on JOHN *sitting with his back against the wall of a trench. There is dim lighting as it is nearing sundown and a fair amount of fog and mist floating about.* JOHN *wears battle gear including dirty and torn fatigues and a chipped and dented helmet. He is covered in mud and grime and lies limply. One might mistake him for dead if he did not blink every few seconds. Most noticeably, there is a large bandage covering part of his midsection. His weapon lays on his lap with no magazine in it. In one of his hands he is clutching a crumpled piece of paper. Next to him, there are empty water bottles and wrappers for food rations along with several spent casings and empty magazines. Also, there is a small radio next to him on the ground, crackling with jumbled and unintelligible speech.* JOHN *sits alone for a few moments, staring blankly ahead. Out of the shadows comes* DEATH. DEATH *is dressed similarly to* JOHN, *wearing combat gear. However, his clothes are clean and neat.* DEATH *approaches* JOHN *and stands before him. He does not sit down.)*

DEATH
Hello, John Conrad.

JOHN
(Looks startled to see DEATH*)* Ben? What are…how can you…you can't be…I don't…I saw you…Ben I saw you die. You can't be here right now. You can't…*(Clutches at the bandage on his midsection and grunts in pain)*

DEATH

I am not Benjamin Murphy. I chose this appearance to make you feel more comfortable.

JOHN

Who are you then? Did you bring help? I'm kind of stuck here.

DEATH

There is nobody else with me. I apologize, John. *(Points to the bandage)* How does the wound in your abdomen feel?

JOHN

It hurts.

DEATH

But the pain is bearable?

JOHN

I think so.

DEATH

Good. I understand that your memory has been damaged. I am here to help guide you. Can you begin by telling me how you received your wound?

JOHN

(Dazed) It's fuzzy. I remember us running.

DEATH

What were you running from? Who was with you?

JOHN

I was with the rest of my squad. We got overrun and had to fall back. Ben got hit and I stopped to grab him. I pulled him as far as I could...

DEATH

And?

JOHN

He was losing blood. I knew he wasn't going to make it even if I got out with him.

DEATH

And yet you stayed with him. But why put your own life at risk?

JOHN

He's my best friend. I couldn't leave without him.

DEATH

He bled to death in your arms.

JOHN

(Nods) But he gave me a paper. He said I had to get it back to base for him. Where did I…I can't remember if I…*(JOHN looks for the paper for a few moments and begins to panic before he realizes he's still holding it)* It was for his brother. He made me promise to get it back for him. He was my best friend. I need to get it back home.

DEATH

What happened to the rest of your friends, John?

JOHN

They left. They kept running when he fell.

DEATH

They abandoned you both. Left you for death.

JOHN

No. They just didn't see me stop. When they realize that I didn't go with them, they'll come back.

DEATH

John, I understand that it may be difficult to accept. But they are not going to come back for you.

JOHN

Yes, they are. They're on their way now.

DEATH

Do you know how long you have been out here, John?

JOHN

(He puts his hand to his head) I don't...know. Maybe a few hours. They'll be back.

DEATH

It has been six days since they left you. No one is coming for you. The wound on your side will be fatal. You are to die here, John. But all will be well.

JOHN

No. No. I just need...I need to...I just...*(Fumbles and grabs the radio next to him. Tries to tune it to get a signal, but all that is heard is more jumbled speech)*

DEATH

They cannot hear you. No one is listening and nobody will come looking for you.

JOHN

(Begins sobbing) No. They are. I think I can hear them trying to respond. They say they're coming. They're on their way already.

DEATH

(Slowly moves his hand toward the radio in JOHN'S *hand. The sounds coming out slowly turn from jumbled and incoherent into the audible speech of his teammates)* Listen, John. You are dead to them already.

(The sound of glasses clinking is heard through the radio. Following is the sound of slurred and drunken voices.)

HANKS

To Benjamin Murphy.

DILLON and MERCER

To Ben!

HANKS

And to John Conrad.

DILLON and MERCER

To John.

DILLON

I'll miss them.

HANKS

We all will.

MERCER

Hell! I'll just miss nailing John at the range. Son of a bitch couldn't shoot for shit. Still owed me a hundred bucks from our last bet.

DILLON

Ben and John are dead, and you're worried about a hundred dollars.

134

MERCER

Whatever. Maybe he had something good stashed in his quarters...

(The radio fades back into jumbled noise.)

JOHN

That isn't real. You're lying.

DEATH

I cannot lie to you. I may show you whatever I wish to convince you, but I am not allowed to be dishonest.

JOHN

I don't know...what that means. Convince me? Who are you? Why are you here?

DEATH

Come with me, John. *(Holds his hand out for* JOHN*)* This hate ridden world is finished with you. It has shown you great misery and suffering. I will take you where you will feel no sorrow. Every tear shall be wiped from your eyes. There will be no more death or mourning or crying or pain, for the old order of things shall pass away.

JOHN

Revelations 21:4. You're an angel.

DEATH

No. I simply take humans home where they belong. You do not belong here any longer, John. You must die and allow me to take you home.

JOHN

(*Upon realizing* DEATH'S *true identity, he puts his hand to his head and, with a gasp, finds that his headache has alleviated. He speaks more clearly and is more perceptive to what is going on around him. He still shows an amount of pain at his wound in his abdomen*) If I'm supposed to die, then why haven't you taken me yet? Why stand here and talk to me?

DEATH

There are rules that I am bound to. As I have previously stated, I am not allowed to lie to you or be dishonest. I am also not allowed to take you without consent. All humans must come with me willingly. Let me help you leave this place of suffering and take you home to your father. Take my hand and then all will be well.

JOHN

(*Slowly reaches for* DEATH'S *hand before recoiling and grasping at the paper*) I can't leave yet.

DEATH

(*Almost frustrated*) Why not?

JOHN

I have to get the note back to base. I promised Ben I would get it back.

DEATH

I spoke to Benjamin. He is in a better place now. He needed much convincing. I will never understand your kind; and your desire to stay in such a wretched place.

JOHN

You talked to Ben? What did he say?

DEATH

He had many kind things to say about you. He honored you as his closest friend. He wanted me to tell you that he is excited to see you again soon. He was also proud of how you behaved in battle. He trained you well. You stopped to come to his aid when all others kept running. Take my hand John and then all will be well. Wouldn't you like to be with your friend again?

(Pause)

JOHN

Did he say anything about the note? *(DEATH does not answer)* What did he say? You said you can't lie to me so tell me what he said.

DEATH

It is of little consequence. You need not worry about it.

JOHN

I want to know. Tell me!

DEATH

We will speak later, John. For the time being you will sleep. *(Puts his hand on JOHN'S forehead and JOHN falls asleep)*

(LIZ enters followed by RON. DEATH crosses his arms and watches the two converse.)

LIZ

For the last time. Stay away from me. You aren't welcome in my home.

RON

Come on, Liz. We both know how lonely you are now that John isn't here. You need a real man to step in now that he's gone. And I'm right here, sweetheart.

LIZ

A real man? Is that what you call yourself? An asshole who peaked in high school and never made anything of himself. One who is now trying to get a woman to cheat on her husband while he's away fighting. Fighting for your freedom and your right to stand here pissing me off.

RON

Well, shit.

LIZ

Stay away from me, Ron.

(Blackout)

Scene Two

(The lights slowly come up with an orange glow, signifying sunrise. DEATH, who previously looked like JOHN'S friend, is now gone, replaced with a new appearance. DEATH now appears as RON but speaks in the same tone and inflection as earlier. DEATH is now dressed in plain clothes. He wears a pair of shorts and a clean polo along with tall socks and sandals. JOHN slowly wakes.)

DEATH

Good morning, John.

JOHN

Hell....Why do you look like Ron now? Could have picked someone with less of their head up their ass....Who the hell even wears socks and sandals.

DEATH

How is your wound feeling?

JOHN

(Grunts in pain) Like it needs a new dressing. *(Points to a wrapping of gauze which sits near* DEATH'S *feet, out of* JOHN'S *reach)* Would you hand me that, at least? I need to change it.

DEATH

I cannot interact physically with objects here.

JOHN

Is that why you picked Ron to look like? So you can be just as big of an asshole? I thought you picked your appearance to make me feel more comfortable. Pick my friends and stuff. Not my asshole neighbors...

DEATH

I apologize. It must have been a mistake. Do you have a girlfriend at home, John?

JOHN

Yeah. Her name is Liz.

DEATH

You miss her, don't you?

JOHN

Of course I do. I was going to try and find a nice job back stateside instead of reenlisting again.

DEATH

You have been an excellent partner to her. You even carry a picture of her in your pocket during your patrols.

JOHN

Yeah. *(Pulls a small wallet-sized picture of her out of his pocket and stares at it)*

(While he stares, LIZ enters unseen to him. She is holding a pregnancy test and has her eyes closed)

JOHN

She's my everything. This is why I have to stay. *(Looks up)* Liz!

DEATH

(Moves and stands next to JOHN, facing LIZ) She can't hear you. This is simply a projection of her. She certainly is very beautiful. Irresistible, even.

JOHN

Why is she holding a pregnancy test?

(LIZ then opens her eyes at the test. She gasps and covers her mouth and begins sobbing.)

JOHN

It's positive? But why is she crying? She was always talking about wanting a little girl. I don't understand. Why are you showing me this?

DEATH

Haven't you always wanted a child?

JOHN

Yes.

DEATH

What would you plan to name your young one?

JOHN

No. You aren't going to start talking and getting me off track to mess with me. I don't feel that headache anymore. Why are you showing this to me?

DEATH

I just don't want the weight of this to be lost in the moment. Speaking of which…look.

(LIZ continues crying and pulls a bottle of Plan B pills out of her pocket and takes one and she slowly begins to calm down.)

JOHN

No! Why would she take that? We've been wanting to….Why would she take that?

DEATH

Because John, *(whispers)* the child wasn't yours.

JOHN

(Stunned for several long beats before slowly gathering himself to speak again. Weakly) Whose child is it?

(Instead of answering, DEATH moves toward LIZ and puts his arm around her shoulder. JOHN then pulls a sidearm out of his holster and begins firing at DEATH. He fires several rounds and keeps trying to fire even after the weapon is empty. DEATH moves back to JOHN and LIZ exits.)

DEATH

There is nothing left in this world for you, John. Not even your beloved Elizabeth.

(JOHN *looks at him and says nothing.*)

DEATH

I want for you to understand that I gain no pleasure in your pain. In fact, I do feel sympathy. Your squad has abandoned you. They left you here to die of your wounds. Does it not feel cold, by the way? The wind is almost biting today; I wonder if a storm will soon approach. And your oh-so-faithful girlfriend. The woman you have loved for several years has, less than a week after your departure, gone behind your back and been impregnated by a man who wears socks with sandals and mows his lawn every other day. *(Beat)* I understand your pain, John. I felt it, too, once. Before I became what I am now. Come with me, John, and I will take you home. Where streets are paved with gold and where the presence of the Lord himself can be felt everywhere. Take my hand, John. Then all will be well.

JOHN

Fuck you, Ron.

(DEATH *sighs and touches* JOHN'S *forehead again, causing a blackout. During the blackout, there are sounds of heavy gunfire and explosions. These sounds go on for a few seconds before becoming background noise to the following dialogue which comes through the same radio.*)

MERCER

Charlie 3 to base! We need air support and evac! Insurgents have overrun our position and we've taken heavy casualties. What's your E.T.A?

(Radio crackling)

HANKS

We aren't getting any backup any time soon! We have to fall back from this position! Charlie squad: check in.

DILLON

Charlie 2 checking in.

MERCER

Charlie 3 checking in.

HANKS

Does anybody have a visual on Conrad or Murphy?

DILLON

I saw Murphy get hit with a stray round, but I don't have a visual.

MERCER

They must have fallen behind. We need to head back for them.

HANKS

Negative. We need to get back to base. We can't hold a position here. Fall back.

DILLON

But we can't just—

HANKS

I said fall back. When we get back to base, we'll send a squad for extraction. But we need to get out of here now. Move out.

Scene Three

(The lights come up faintly as it is nighttime in the trench with great sounds of wind and an incoming storm. DEATH now looks like his true

self. He wears a black cloak and has no face but a skull. His voice this time is much more deep and demon-like. He is to look very vile and disgusting, even compared to JOHN. JOHN *is still asleep when the lights come up.* DEATH *moves toward* JOHN *to speak to him but is startled by something offstage. He grimaces and fades into the shadows.* ENEMY *enters.* ENEMY *wears a combat uniform but notably bears the medic insignia on his helmet and armband. Like* JOHN, *he is also very dirty and worn. He notices* JOHN *on the ground, asleep, and levels his weapon at him.)*

ENEMY

Merde…*(Wakes* JOHN*)*

JOHN

Shit….Get out of here, you goddamn Franc. I'm finished, already.

ENEMY

Parlez-vous Francais?

JOHN

Didn't you hear me, Franc? Go back to Paris.

ENEMY

Ta blessure a mauvaise mine. Je peux aider.

JOHN

I said get the fuck out of here! You killed me. I'm never going home, and you killed me.

ENEMY

Quelle est cette note? *(Toward the note)*

JOHN

Note?

ENEMY

Oui. La note.

JOHN

I need to get it back home. For my friend.

ENEMY

Friend. Ton amis.

JOHN

Can you take it back to your base? They'll send it to the
address. Take it to your…what's the word…maison. Take
'note' to 'maison'. Understand? Oui? *(Gives the note to* ENEMY*)*

ENEMY

Oui. Je vais le livrer.

JOHN

Thank you. Thank you…

ENEMY

*(Goes to exit but stops. He pulls a small syringe out of his backpack and
gives it to* JOHN*)* Morphine. Pour ta blessure.

JOHN

(Takes the syringe and injects it. He sighs with relief) Thank you,
Franc. Um…merci.

ENEMY

De rien. *(Exits)*

DEATH

(Enters from the shadows) Excellent. The letter shall now return
and your duty has been fulfilled. Now that the matter is
resolved, you will come with me?

JOHN

No.

DEATH

And why is that? Your letter is gone and thus your final burden has been lifted. Your death is near, John. You cannot stop that. Come with me.

JOHN

I just....I don't want to die.

DEATH

(Yelling) You insignificant, shortsighted mortal! I have no more patience for you. You will die in this trench where you sit. You cannot stop this, John Conrad.

JOHN

I just don't want to die, okay? You wouldn't understand. I know what's here for me. Life is shitty sometimes, but at least I know it's real and that it makes sense. Besides, you said you can't make me go. So I can't die if I stay here.

DEATH

Why won't you understand that I am only trying to help you? I am trying to save your soul from an eternity of this suffering and misery. Even if you could stay here, there is nothing left here for you. Your closest and only true friend has already died. The love of your life has been with another man since the day you left. Your team has abandoned you, and that bullet in your side is spreading the worst kind of poison throughout your body. If the infection doesn't kill you, then the elements will. You must choose to come with me in order to leave this earth. If you refuse, you will not heal and recover. Instead, you will stay here, your body will still die, and your spirit will remain in torment. You will be stranded for all of eternity. Your soul will leave your body and will be forever bound to the spot where you died. It will be forced to stay in this wretched place and see the flesh of your face decay and rot from your skull and be devoured by maggots as your mind slowly gives and your spirit goes mad from isolation. Your spirit will for the rest of time feel the same emotional and physical pain that you feel at this moment with no rest and relief. *(Beat)* Do you feel that? That was the first raindrop before a great storm arrives. The temperature is now below freezing, and your body temperature is now nearing 89 degrees. You have lost much blood already. If you are lucky, then maybe a lightning strike will kill you quickly. If not, then your body will slowly die from the cold as each one of your organs shuts down one by one until you finally give up the ghost. You will not survive this night, John Conrad. *(His tone softens)* You must make your decision. You must come with me. Take my hand. And then all will be well.

(JOHN looks toward the wound on his abdomen and cringes at the pain of it. DEATH holds out his hand and JOHN slowly takes it as the lights slowly fade out.)

DEATH
And then all will be well.

(The lights come up on JOHN alone on stage. He is on his knees and holds his head down. The lights shift from neutral to a cool blue. He holds his head up and looks toward the light in fear. The lights then fade out.)

MIDWESTERN VAMPIRE

CHARACTERS

Vlad

Barkeep

Rider

Angel

(Lights up. VLAD is sitting in the back corner of the room, keeping to himself as the BARKEEP is wiping dishes.)

BARKEEP
You plan on ordering a drink, fella?

VLAD
Not quite yet. *(To himself)* I'm waiting for the right one.

BARKEEP
Everything you can see is all that we got. Either order something or get out. Didn't you read the sign? No loitering.

VLAD
It will just be a while longer. The sun still lurks across the sky.

BARKEEP

And it will again tomorrow! Freak.

(RIDER *makes a harsh entrance, rather trying to make a statement coming into the saloon.* VLAD *immediately watches him intently, and his eyes follow* RIDER *as he approaches the bar.*)

BARKEEP

What will it be, friend?

RIDER

Whiskey. No ice.

VLAD

(To himself) That's the one.

BARKEEP

You could have said that earlier! Two whiskeys, no ice.

(RIDER *is uneasy. He appears to be rather suspicious of* VLAD. BARKEEP *pours the drinks and sets them on the counter.* RIDER *picks up the glasses and walks to* VLAD, *who mistakenly ordered a drink.*)

VLAD

Go ahead and drink mine. *(To himself)* I'll enjoy it more later.

RIDER

Stranger. If I drink it, it's gone. *(Awkward silence)* You aren't from around here are you?

VLAD

Are any of us truly from where we claim? Our origins have been skewed in our lineage. Generation after generation, traveling place to place. Farther from understanding who we truly are.

RIDER

Sir, I popped out my mama right here in Muskogee.

VLAD

You people. So ignorant. Never willing to open your minds. Spoon-fed how to think your whole lives, never questioning why things are the way they are. Abiding by the ideas embedded in you that were originally crafted by the minds of brilliant men long ago.

RIDER

Yep, you're definitely one of them northerners. I can tell because your skin is so pale.

VLAD

Why do I waste my time with you pathetic people?

(RIDER *suddenly spits his whiskey on* VLAD *who falls back in pain. It's as if* RIDER *were an entirely different man.*)

RIDER

Garlic salts.

(VLAD *is coughing on the floor.* BARKEEP, *frightened by the commotion, draws a gun from under the bar.*)

BARKEEP

Whatever this is, take it outside, or I'm getting the sheriff.

RIDER

Leave.

(Silence. VLAD rises and darts behind RIDER while he is focused on the BARKEEP.)

RIDER

If you enjoy your life, then you'll leave. This is a matter of dark forces that you wouldn't understand.

BARKEEP

Well, if you explain it slowly, maybe I'll be able to follow your opinion, and, in return, I'll tell you what I think. Conversation is the best way to compromise and learn…

RIDER

Get out!

(The BARKEEP runs out the door. RIDER turns to finish VLAD and sees he is no longer there. VLAD pins RIDER to the table.)

VLAD

My only wish was to repress my eternal thirst by selecting a single individual to drain as I journey across the western landmass of this world, but you made this personal.

RIDER

Hold it! If you're truly on a quest across the western plains, since you are immortal, it's presumably to acquire knowledge. Ain't I right, blood sucker?

VLAD

What knowledge could you possibly possess for me?

RIDER

I'm trained. I track, hunt, and kill your kind. That's impressive, for a human. You must wonder what I know so you can be ready for the next time you come across another hunter.

VLAD

(To himself) The mortal appears to think of more than trivial concepts. Perhaps I should dissect his mind; unraveling the corpse kept in wraps of human ideals. Unstacking the Russian dolls of his brain, picking out the seed of all his secrets.

RIDER

Hey! End monologue. Do we have a deal?

VLAD

(Lets go and walks away steadily, eyeballing him every step) How did you access the garlic salts whilst containing whiskey within your maw?

RIDER

I have raised chipmunks on a farm in southern Nebraska, north of Norton in Kansas. I have gotten to study their habits and abilities.

VLAD

(To himself) A bewildering creature, perhaps he is worth sparing. Mayhaps I will test his knowledge in the dark arts. Then I'll truly know…

RIDER

You want me to do magic?

VLAD

A mind interpreter! Extraordinary.

RIDER

You're talking out loud, it's not hard to….

VLAD

My intelligence insulted by a mere mortal! These words will be the last to pass your lips, for I will…

RIDER

I know magic.

VLAD

What?

RIDER

If I prove to you that I know magic, will you let me live?

VLAD

(To himself) Magic. An unexplainable construct to alter the matter encaptured around our very being.

RIDER

(Sighs) Here we go again.

VLAD

(Continuing) I have explored all of Western Europe, and never have I had the pleasure of an entanglement with a being conducting the unfathomable. You have me intrigued.

RIDER

So *(Picks up the glass from the table)* I am going…

(ANGEL enters door in between the two characters and remains in front of the entry.)

ANGEL

Stop!

VLAD

(Hisses) Not a divine one.

ANGEL

Mortal, you mustn't engage with a dark one, or…

(RIDER *holds up his finger as a gun and pops his thumb down, causing the* ANGEL *to "vanish." * ANGEL *backs out through doorway.*)

VLAD

(Awed) How?! An earthbound meat sack obliviate the eternal?

RIDER

I don't believe in angels.

VLAD

The statement which you orchestrated is absurd. The harmonious demon was standing right there!

RIDER

Listen. You can believe what you want. I'll believe what I want. We all have the right to our own opinions.

VLAD

We can't opinion elements out of existence!

RIDER

That's your opinion.

VLAD

(To himself) This man has performed an act my eyes have never beheld. The interaction of a plethora of mystical creatures and none, not even Dracula, has completed that feat.

RIDER

Am I free to go?

VLAD

I believe you are. *(Beat)* I believe…I'm human.

(Blackout)

The Jeanne Lobmeyer Cárdenas Prize in Short Fiction & The Sr. Madeleine Kisner Prize in Poetry

The Jeanne Lobmeyer Cárdenas Prize in Short Fiction and the Sr. Madeleine Kisner Prize in Poetry is awarded each year. Journal staff members handle preliminary judging, and all submissions accepted for publication are considered. Winners are then selected by distinguished, nationally-recognized writers. Past judges have included Michael Arnzen, Doris Betts, Bruce Bond, Scott Cairns, Marta Ferguson, Lise Goett, Albert Goldbarth, Jeanine Hathaway, Laura Kopchick, David Lunde, Paul Mariani, P. Andrew Miller, Christopher Moore, Virginia Stem Owens, Timothy Richardson, Barbara Rodman, Vicky Lee Santiesteban, Philip Schneider, Tim Seibles, Richard Spilman, Sonya Taaffe, Jeanne Murray Walker, Albert Wendland, Ned Balbo, Douglas Ford, and Marge Simon.

Jeanne Lobmeyer Cárdenas

Jeanne Lobmeyer Cárdenas, Professor Emeritus at Newman University, received her Bachelor's degree from Sacred Heart College (now Newman University) and her Master's degree from Marquette University. An award-winning press writer, Professor Cárdenas taught literature, writing, and journalism at Newman, imparting her passion for language to students. The Jeanne Lobmeyer Cárdenas Prize in Short Fiction continues Professor Cárdenas' influence on the careers of student writers.

Sister Madeleine Kisner

Sr. Madeleine Kisner, A.S.C., held a Bachelor's degree from Sacred Heart College (Newman University), a Master's degree from Creighton, and a Doctor of Art from the University of Michigan. A published poet and writer, Sr. Madeleine taught her students both the music and the craft of words during her twenty-year teaching career at Newman. Sadly, Sr. Madeleine has passed, but the Kisner Prize in Poetry continues her work with future generations of poets.

2020 WINNERS & RUNNERS UP

Poetry

Winner: Target at 7:40 a.m.   Nathan Yeager
Runner Up: Don Rockwell   Joseph Mick

Prose

Winner: Smash the Car   Cole Schnieders
Runner Up: The Weight of a Name   Madeline Alvarez

2020 FINALISTS

Poetry

Red Grow the Lilies	Madeline Alvarez
Black Beach	Matthew D. Clark
Malam	Kristin Lau
Autumn Thoughts	Ashley Nguyen
Far From Home	Steven Nguyen
Dove	Kaitlyn Smith
Grey Area	Allison Williams

Prose

Earth & Air	Matthew D. Clark
Sindbad Sings the Blues	Adam Steffens

Prose Judge—Douglas Ford

Douglas Ford lives and works on the west coast of Florida, just off an exit made famous by a Jack Ketchum short story. He is the author of the upcoming collection of weird fiction, Ape in the Ring and Other Tales of the Macabre and Uncanny. His work has appeared in Dark Moon Digest, Infernal Ink, Weird City, along with The Best Hardcore Horror, Volumes Three and Four. His Stoker-recommended novella, The Reattachment, appeared in 2019 courtesy of Madness Heart Press. In the harsh light of day, he sprinkles a little darkness into the lives of his students at the State College of Florida, and he lives with a Hovawart (that's a kind of dog) who fiercely protects him from the unseen creatures living in the wooded area next to his house. His three cats merely tolerate him, but his wife is decidedly fond of him, as he is of her.

Poetry Judge—Tim Richardson

Tim Richardson's poems have appeared in The Paris Review, North American Review, Western Humanities Review, and Barely South Review, among other journals. He is the author of Contingency, Immanence, and the Subject of Rhetoric (2013, Parlor Press) and is Associate Professor of English at the University of Texas at Arlington, where he teaches courses in writing, media, and theory.

SUBMISSIONS

Coelacanth accepts submissions from all university undergraduates. The journal is published annually. Writers may send short stories, novel excerpts, poetry, plays, and creative nonfiction manuscripts to either of the following addresses:

COELACANTH
c/o Bryan D. Dietrich
Newman University
3100 W McCormick ST
Wichita, KS 67213-2008

NewmanCoelacanth@gmail.com

Rejected manuscripts will not be replied to or returned unless accompanied by a self-addressed, stamped envelope. All submissions must be in English and previously unpublished.

Simultaneous submissions are acceptable, provided authors give immediate notification of publication in other media. Please include phone and email contact information. Authors and artists retain all rights to their work(s) as those works appear in the journal. Prospective authors should read earlier volumes of *Coelacanth* to acquaint themselves with material the journal has already published. Back issues may be obtained by writing to either of the addresses above.